For my mother, always.

THE MEDITERRANEAN COOK

Meni Valle

A year of seasonal eating

Smith Street Books

SPRING — SUMMER

22

AUTUMN — WINTER

124

I t was summertime and my first visit to Greece. I went to see where my parents were born and meet family who I had only met through the letters and gifts they had posted to me in Australia.

My *thea* (aunty) Sophia was standing outside, waiting for me. She lived in a small cottage on the edge of town in the region of Florina. The house was in a tiny court off the main road, with a small, grassed area in the middle and a single park bench.

We walked into her home arm in arm, through the kitchen and out to the back porch where we sat on the steps overlooking her vegetable garden. As we rested, the sun cast a warm glow over the garden and the plants seemed to come alive in the golden light. We sat, ate, drank tea and I listened to her stories. There were moments of tears and others of laughter but all the time there was a feeling of love and connection. There was so much to catch up on.

Walking through thea Sophia's garden we started chatting about the vegetables she grew, and she explained that she didn't eat anything she hadn't grown herself. I soon discovered this was important to her in many ways. She told me that she had learned how to grow vegetables from her mother, my grandmother. She then smiled and said that gardening is not only good for the body but for the mind, too – the fresh air, the plants, the connection to nature. One of the best things we can do for ourselves is to eat locally produced, preferably organic, seasonal food as much as we can, which, of course, she did every day.

For thea Sophia, growing fresh produce wasn't just a hobby, it was a way of life. Once a week, she would go to the market for a little fish or meat, cheese, pulses and grains, and perhaps some bread if she hadn't been able to bake her own that week, and then pair these simple ingredients with fresh vegetables from her garden.

Next to the vegetable garden sat thea Sophia's outdoor kitchen, her *magereio*. Separated from the main house, it was only one room but it resembled a tiny house all of its own, and it was where thea Sophia liked to cook, pickle and preserve the summer produce that would see her through the winter months. Herbs hung drying in bunches next to strings of onions and peppers (capsicums) and plaited garlic – it was a place of hands-on hard work, but it was also a space where food rituals were created and treasured … a magical sanctuary, just for my aunt.

My most precious memories of thea Sophia are of the time we spent in her tiny kitchen, overlooking her vegetable garden. As we cooked together, she recounted stories from her childhood and her memories of my mother as a young girl. My mother had spent most of her younger years growing up and living in Thessaloniki, and this was reflected in her cooking. Her meals were not only influenced by geography, but also from the kitchens of the Ottoman, Sephardic Jews, Slavs and other communities who lived in the region, and she loved making sophisticated and refined dishes as much as she did filo pies. Like my mother, thea Sophia was an outstanding cook as well.

❉

My passion for food lies in home cooking and especially that of the Mediterranean. It is the food of my childhood, the food I cook for my own family, as well as the dishes I have discovered during my travels. They are all made using ingredients that are familiar to me – I cannot imagine my kitchen without lemons, olive oil, tomatoes, herbs, spices and peppers.

The food of the Mediterranean is often thought of as simple, but I believe it is sophisticated, with rich and refined dishes. Either way, it is always generous.

This book invites you into my kitchen, to share in the recipes I hold dear and that have played a role in my life. Within the recipes, you will find tips for using leftovers, ideas for pairing meals and advice on how to pick the best fruit and vegetables.

I hope you make the dishes in this book and then make them your own, find the joy brought by each new season's produce and feel confident to get creative. These are the recipes that I love and, for me, what the Mediterranean way of life is all about: sharing good food and stories with loved ones around the dinner table! I hope they become a part of your kitchen and that you love them as much as I do.

AN ODE TO THE
MEDITERRANEAN DIET

The Mediterranean diet is a way of eating based on the traditional foods and cooking techniques of countries that border the Mediterranean Sea. It involves a diet of plenty of fresh fruits and vegetables, legumes and whole grains, as well as healthy fats such as olive oil, nuts and seeds. Fish and seafood are also important components of the Mediterranean diet, as are moderate amounts of cheese and yoghurt. Red meat is only eaten in small quantities and alcohol is generally only served with food and always with company.

While the food is important, the lifestyle that accompanies it is equally so. The Mediterranean lifestyle is characterised by regular physical activity, such as walking and gardening, socialising and spending time with loved ones, a sense of community and a slower pace of life, allowing time for rest and connections. It is a holistic approach to health and wellness.

MY MEDITERRANEAN KITCHEN

The Mediterranean pantry consists of an ever-ready supply of ingredients that allow you to put together a meal at a moment's notice, so when friends pop in unexpectedly it's easy to throw together a meze plate of olives, cheese and pickles, served with bread.

Here are the ingredients that are always in my pantry; ingredients that you shouldn't be without. They are the starting point of my recipes and have helped make me the cook that I am. They are probably familiar to most of you and can be easily found at your local store or market.

BREAD

As an essential part of the Mediterranean pantry, bread holds a special place. Every country has their own traditional loaf: focaccias and ciabattas from Italy; country loaves from Greece; flatbreads from the North African coast and up into Israel; rustic pa de pages and the elongated pan de cristal from Catalonia; and baguettes from France are a fundamental part of the Mediterranean table and culture. These breads add diversity and character to the Mediterranean kitchen. From soaking up sauces, scooping dips or blitzing into breadcrumbs, they play a crucial role in the Mediterranean way of life.

My go-to bread is sourdough, with its ancient fermentation techniques and natural flavour, it complements so many of the dishes I like to cook. Olive bread is also a favourite, served alongside pickles and cheese, and perhaps a small glass of wine.

CAPERS

Despite their small size, capers are tiny flavour bombs, packing an explosive punch of taste that can transform even the simplest of dishes into something extraordinary. I love scattering them over salads and roasted vegetables, or dicing finely and adding to dressings. Capers are generally sold pickled in brine or salted.

CHEESE

Greek feta is non-negotiable in my kitchen and many of the dishes in this book are served with this salty and tangy cheese alongside, perhaps with some crusty bread. PDO Greek feta follows strict specifications and must be made with at least 70 per cent sheep's milk, with the remainder made up of goat's milk, and stored in brine. I love to add feta to pies and omelettes, or crumble it over pasta, roasted vegetables and salads.

Other cheeses I always have on hand include mozzarella and parmesan (always freshly grated), and at times, for a little indulgence, dreamy burrata, ricotta and cheddar.

GARLIC

A member of the allium family, garlic is a culinary dynamo that can elevate the simplest of dishes. I have memories of my mother growing garlic in her garden. Once fully matured, she would harvest the garlic, carefully braid the long stalks together and hang them up to cure in a cool, dry place. My mother took great care in this centuries-old practice, which not only creates a beautiful display but, for me, evokes memories of traditional rituals.

GRAINS & LEGUMES

I cannot overstate the importance of grains and legumes in the Mediterranean diet. They have been cultivated throughout the region for thousands of years and feature heavily in dishes from Spain and France to Italy, Greece and Turkey, providing protein and fibre in lieu of a diet rich in red meat. I prefer to use dried beans and lentils, but when time is short, or I haven't had the opportunity to plan a meal in advance, tinned legumes are a saviour, ready to be whipped out and added to soups and salads, or used as a blank canvas for which to add flavour.

Pasta and rice (short-grain, arborio, long-grain) are also necessities in the Mediterranean kitchen when creating a stand-alone dish. A simple plate of pasta tossed in butter and served with feta crumbled over the top is, for me, a hug in a bowl.

GREEK-STYLE YOGHURT

Yoghurt is a breakfast staple in Greece, but it is also added to cakes, pies and dressings, and used in place of mayonnaise and sour cream, throughout the Mediterranean. Greek-style yoghurt is made by straining the extra whey found in regular yoghurt, making it thicker, creamier and a little tangier.

I always buy full-fat Greek-style yoghurt. It has less sugar and more protein than regular yoghurt, making it a healthier choice.

HERBS & SPICES

I grew up in a house where my mother grew most of her own herbs. Oregano was an essential, which she would dutifully harvest from the garden in summer and hang upside down to dry, ready to be used in dishes in the following months. Perhaps, unsurprisingly, dried oregano is a regular feature in my kitchen, along with thyme, parsley, dill and mint, the latter of which is especially easy to grow at home. When it comes to spices, I use paprika, cinnamon, nutmeg, saffron, cumin and coriander to add complexity and warmth to dishes. Some of the recipes in this book ask for a little more of a spice than you might be used to adding, but, trust me, the extra makes all the difference.

HONEY

The natural sweetness of honey makes it a versatile and, for me, indispensable ingredient in the Mediterranean pantry. In cooking I add it to salad dressings, pastries and desserts, and I love to drizzle a spoonful into my herbal tea, or over some Greek-style yoghurt topped with walnuts for breakfast or a snack any time of the day.

Honey also pairs beautifully with fresh fruits and is luscious over savoury pies (see page 82) and with cheeses. I like to buy honey in bulk as it has no expiration date and will keep indefinitely in a cool, dark place.

LEMONS

An essential in any Mediterranean pantry, lemon juice enhances the flavour of sauces, dips, dressings, roasted veg, freshly cooked fish, desserts and so much more. If you have an overabundance of lemons, or are lucky enough to have a lemon tree in your garden, I highly recommend freezing the juice to give you a year-round supply of fresh citrus. Simply measure out and strain the juice into ice-cube trays, then transfer to a zip-lock bag, once frozen, for easier storage. Frozen lemon juice keeps well for up to 4 months – don't forget to label and date the bag.

NUTS & SEEDS

Almonds, walnuts, pine nuts, sesame seeds ...
In dishes and as a snack, nuts and seeds are
enjoyed throughout the Mediterranean, adding
textural diversity, as well as being a rich source
of healthy fats and nutrients.

I always use raw nuts and toast them myself,
as I love their enhanced flavour. I recommend
toasting nuts and seeds separately as their cooking
times vary. For nuts, place them in a drying
frying pan over medium heat and toast, stirring
constantly and watching them closely in case
they start to burn, for 4–6 minutes, until darkened
slightly and aromatic with a shiny appearance.
Seeds will take 1–2 minutes. Once toasted,
immediately remove the nuts and seeds from the
frying pan to prevent further cooking and burning.

OLIVE OIL

Without olive oil, my food wouldn't be the same.
It is the centrepiece of Mediterranean cuisine and has
been an integral part of my cooking since childhood.
I can't imagine preparing a meal without it.

The difference between olive oil and extra
virgin is that regular olive oil is heated to extract
the oil and then refined, whereas extra virgin olive
oil is cold-pressed and left unrefined. It usually has
a stronger, fruitier flavour and is darker in colour.

Typically, olive oil is better suited to
sauteing, roasting, braising and baking because
of its higher smoke point and neutral flavour.
Extra virgin olive oil is ideal for flavourful
vinaigrettes and drizzling over finished dishes.

OLIVES

Whether served on a meze platter, enjoyed as a snack with an aperitif, or added to salads or stews, olives, with their delightful pops of saltiness, feature heavily throughout Mediterranean cuisines. I always have at least a couple of varieties in my fridge or pantry, with green Sicilian olives and black kalamata olives in brine or salt being my favourites. Sicilian olives are celebrated for their aromatic and fruity flavour, while kalamata olives boast a luscious, fruity taste with a subtle hint of bitterness.

The flavour profile and texture of olives varies depending on where they come from and how they are prepared, so experiment to see which ones you love best.

PICKLED VEGETABLES

I am a huge fan of pickled vegetables and they are always on rotation in my kitchen. I adore experimenting with different vegetables and aromatics, but I also have tried-and-tested favourites that I return to again and again (see pages 98–113). The process of pickling is a joy for me, from preparing the vegetables, herbs and spices, to making the brine with vinegar, water, salt and sugar.

Pickled vegetables are wonderful on a meze plate, served in salads, or as a side to a main meal, to add freshness and zing.

TINNED FISH

Tinned anchovies and sardines are a cherished part of the Mediterranean pantry; an easy way to add flavour to dishes, as well as a quick snack on toast. They are delicious added to pasta sauces and salad dressings for an umami boost, as well as being an integral ingredient in antipasto platters. Not only does tinned fish have a long shelf life, it is an excellent source of heart-healthy omega-3 fatty acids and B12.

TINNED TOMATOES

Fresh tomatoes are perfect during midsummer, but outside this season tinned tomatoes are the workhorse of the Mediterranean kitchen. As winter nears its end and fresh vegetables become scarce, tinned tomatoes are a saviour, adding a lively tartness to soups, braises and pasta sauces.

I mostly use whole tinned tomatoes, so I can either chop them into smaller pieces to create a smoother sauce, or leave them whole for a chunkier texture in roasts.

VINEGARS

I always have a variety of vinegars in my pantry to create flavourful vinaigrettes. Balsamic vinegar adds a rich, sweet tanginess to dressings, while apple cider vinegar is refreshing and slightly fruity. Red wine vinegar brings its bold, robust taste and sherry vinegar is full-flavoured and woodsy. White balsamic is a milder and slightly sweeter version of the traditional balsamic, and a personal favourite of mine. I love to add a little honey or dijon mustard to my vinaigrettes, but I encourage you to experiment with different ingredients and create your own unique combinations, not only for dressing salads but also for drizzling over roasted vegetables.

In addition to vinaigrettes, vinegars are also indispensable for pickling vegetables and to balance and brighten soups and stews.

COOK'S NOTES

STERILISING JARS

To sterilise your jars, wash them in hot soapy water and rinse well, then place them upright in a baking dish and transfer to a cold oven. Heat the oven to 110°C (230°F) fan-forced and leave the jars in the oven for 10–15 minutes, once the oven has reached its temperature, or until completely dry. Remove the jars carefully and allow to cool.

To sterilise the lids, place them in a large saucepan of boiling water for 5 minutes, then drain and dry with paper towels, or leave them on a wire rack to air-dry. Make sure both the jars and lids are completely dry before using.

OVEN TEMPERATURES

The recipes in this book use fan-forced oven temperatures. If you have a conventional oven, increase the oven temperature by 20°C (35°F).

MEASUREMENTS

All relevant ingredients are measured using standard US/UK 15 ml (½ fl oz) tablespoons. If you have a 20 ml tablespoon, reduce the amount by 1 teaspoon. All cups are equal to 250 ml (8½ fl oz).

SPRING — SUMMER

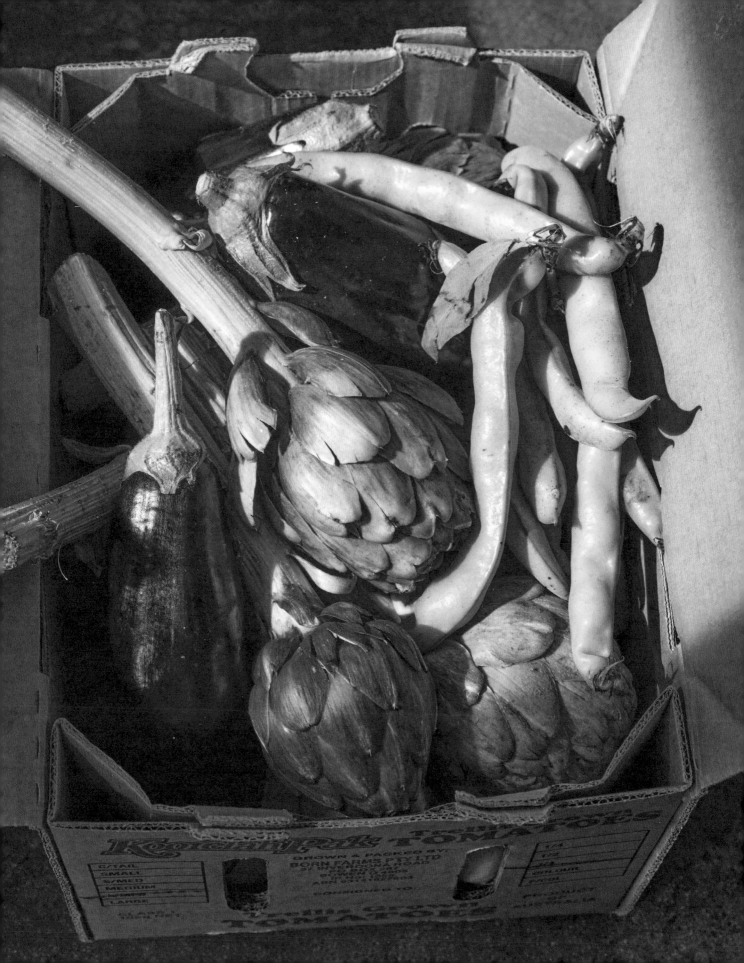

The days are changing and spring is on its way, with its promise of sunny days and sultry evenings. The morning air is still crisp, but the afternoon sun begins to shine with more warmth. We put aside our thick coats, spring-clean our homes and look forward to the joys of the new season's produce: artichokes, tender peas, sweet strawberries and bouquets of crisp asparagus and radish. In the kitchen, hearty dishes are replaced with salads, grilled vegetables and fresh fruits.

As spring gives way to summer, produce becomes more colourful: beautiful red tomatoes, verdant basil and purple eggplants (aubergines), as well as zucchini (courgettes), peppers (capsicums), beetroot (beets) and green beans fill my table, ready to be transformed into something simple but always delicious. For dessert, nothing more is needed than slices of crisp red watermelon, ripe stone fruits or vibrant berries.

My mind thinks back to the local market in the village on the outskirts of Florina in Northern Greece, wandering past stalls with my cousin, Antoni, and his wife, Eleni, hand-woven wicker baskets in hand that we bought from the Romani. There was no need for a list of things to buy; the produce and my cousin were my guide. Eleni knew which stall holders had the ripest tomatoes, the finest zucchini ... 'perhaps not today; next week's will be better'.

As we walked home, our baskets overflowing with produce, we chatted about what to prepare for lunch. The green beans were perfect, so we decided on fasolakia. We set the table outside, overlooking the vegetable garden, and I stopped to feel the gentle breeze on my skin, the sun and its warmth. The rest of the family joined us and another cousin, who lives next door, came too. As I soaked up the calming atmosphere, I was reminded once again of the importance of these small moments of joy. Cooking that meal with my cousin and Eleni will always be in my heart, an experience to forever cherish.

ARTICHOKES & BROAD BEANS WITH LEMON

The artichoke is one of the first vegetables to emerge after winter, bringing its earthy, slightly sweet flavour and tender texture to our kitchens. There are so many ways to cook artichokes: you can grill (broil) or roast them, add them to risottos, stuff with breadcrumbs and so much more. They are a true delight. This artichoke and broad bean dish incorporates my favourite way to cook them, served simply with a squeeze of lemon juice.

✳

Half-fill a large bowl with cold water and add a tablespoon of the lemon juice.

Working with one artichoke at a time, break off the stem and trim the base and top, then remove the tough outer leaves. Use a teaspoon to scoop out the chokes, leaving a cup-shaped artichoke heart. Place in the lemon water to prevent discolouration, then repeat with the remaining artichokes.

Heat the olive oil in a saucepan over medium heat and saute the onion and garlic for 4–5 minutes, until soft. Add the artichoke hearts, broad beans and dill, and season well with salt and pepper. Pour in 375 ml (1½ cups) of water and simmer for 30 minutes or until the vegetables are tender and the sauce has reduced.

Remove the pan from the heat and stir through the remaining lemon juice. Transfer to a large plate and serve. Alternatively, omit the lemon juice and serve the vegetables with a generous amount of avgolemono sauce.

Serves 4

juice of 2 lemons
8 artichokes (you can also use frozen artichoke hearts)
60 ml (¼ cup) olive oil
1 onion, finely diced
2 garlic cloves, minced
750 g (1 lb 11 oz) podded broad (fava) beans
2 tablespoons dill fronds, finely chopped
salt and pepper, to taste
Avgolemono sauce (see page 128), to serve (optional)

Note   *It is not a Mediterranean kitchen if there are no lemons. They enhance the flavour of your food – just a little squeeze of lemon juice can brighten up and balance flavours in a transformative way, bringing a dish to life.*

ROASTED RED PEPPER & WALNUT DIP

Sweet, slightly smoky and a little spicy, this roasted red pepper and walnut dip is similar to Spanish romesco sauce. I love to serve it with fresh or toasted bread, as part of a meze platter or spooned over roasted vegetables or chicken.

❊

Preheat the oven to 200°C (400°F) fan-forced.

Place the peppers on a baking tray and roast, turning occasionally, for 30 minutes or until they are blackened. Remove from the oven and allow to cool, then peel and remove the seeds. Finely chop the flesh and set aside.

Place the garlic in a mortar and use the pestle to grind the garlic to a paste. Pound in the walnuts, a few at a time, drizzling in the olive oil as you go, until you have a chunky paste. Stir through the finely chopped peppers, cumin, cayenne pepper and smoked paprika, and season to taste with salt and pepper. Drizzle with a little red wine vinegar to taste.

Spoon out the dip into a serving bowl and drizzle with a little extra olive oil. Top with a few mint leaves and serve.

Serves 4

3 red peppers (capsicums)
2 garlic cloves
120 g (4½ oz) toasted walnuts
120 ml (4 fl oz) olive oil, plus extra
    to serve
¼ teaspoon ground cumin
¼ teaspoon cayenne pepper
½ teaspoon smoked paprika
salt and pepper, to taste
red wine vinegar, to taste
mint leaves, to serve

28

Make ahead   *The red peppers can be roasted up to two days ahead and kept in an airtight container in the fridge. Allow to come to room temperature before making the dip.*

BOUYOURDI

This moreish dish is found in Thessaloniki, the second-largest city in Greece and a designated City of Gastronomy by UNESCO. Some say that it travelled to Thessaloniki from Smyrna (modern-day Izmir in Turkey), where the cuisine is richer and spicier.

This dish is so much more than baked feta; it is soft, gooey and picante. I like to add kasseri for more depth of flavour – slice the cheese, break it into chunks or crumble as you prefer, and don't leave out the chilli … it is a must. Served with fresh bread to scoop up all the deliciousness, this is my idea of a perfect meze lunch.

❄

Preheat the oven to 200°C (400°F).

Heat the olive oil in a small flameproof casserole dish (Dutch oven) over medium heat, add the garlic and saute for 2 minutes. Add the grated tomato flesh and pepper, and stir well to combine.

Remove the dish from the heat, top with the sliced tomato and season well with salt and pepper. Scatter the kasseri on top, then add the slab of feta, oregano and chilli flakes. Bake for 15–20 minutes, until soft and golden.

Serve with crusty bread.

Serves 4

60 ml (¼ cup) olive oil
2 garlic cloves, minced
3 tomatoes, grated, plus 1 tomato
    extra, sliced
4 sweet long peppers (capsicums),
    halved lengthways and sliced into
    half moons
salt and pepper, to taste
100 g (3½ oz) kasseri cheese
    (if you can't find kasseri, use
    gruyere or an aged cheddar),
    broken into chunks
250 g (9 oz) piece of Greek feta
1 teaspoon dried oregano
½ teaspoon chilli flakes
crusty bread, to serve

31

ZUCCHINI, FETA & MINT OMELETTE

A favourite brunch or light lunch dish, this springtime omelette is light, fluffy and completely delicious. Green peas, asparagus and other spring vegetables also make a wonderful omelette, so feel free to swap out the zucchini for whatever is in abundance at the market.

❄

Place the zucchini in a colander, sprinkle with salt and leave to drain for 20–30 minutes. Squeeze out the excess liquid from the zucchini.

Heat the olive oil in a 24 cm (9½ in) frying pan over medium heat. Add the spring onion and zucchini and saute for about 5 minutes, then add the chopped mint and season well with salt and pepper.

Whisk the eggs and yoghurt in a bowl, then pour the mixture into the frying pan. Using a spatula, push the side of the egg mixture towards the middle, creating space for some of the liquid to fill and cook by tilting the pan. Cook the omelette for 2–3 minutes, until almost set, then slide the omelette onto a plate and fold it over (it will continue to cook for a minute or two and should be slightly soft in the centre).

Crumble the feta over the omelette, scatter with the extra mint leaves and serve.

Serves 4

600 g (1 lb 5 oz) zucchini (courgettes), finely sliced into rounds
salt and pepper, to taste
3 tablespoons olive oil
4 spring onions (scallions), finely chopped
1 tablespoon finely chopped mint leaves, plus extra leaves to serve
6 eggs
2 tablespoons Greek-style yoghurt
100 g (3½ oz) Greek feta

Goes with *Serve this omelette with the Braised tomatoes and peppers on page 45 – the sweet tomatoey pepper sauce pairs perfectly with the zucchini and feta, and makes a gorgeous breakfast or simple meal for any time of the day.*

HOW TO PREPARE
AN ARTICHOKE

This marvellous edible flower is an ancient plant native to the Mediterranean. Whoever persevered to establish the edibility of the artichoke, peeling back the tough outer layers to reveal the tender inner leaves and heart that lie at the centre of this vegetable, we will never know, but I, for one, am grateful for the cultivation of this unlikely hero and its inclusion in the Mediterranean kitchen.

When buying artichokes, look for flowers with tightly closed petals that are firm to the touch and feel a little heavy. Stored properly, fresh artichokes will keep in the fridge for up to 5 days. Leave the heads unwashed, as rinsing them can cause the petals to spoil faster. Instead, simply sprinkle the stems with a little water to keep them from dehydrating, then place in a plastic bag and store in the fridge.

When you are ready to prepare your artichokes, start by filling a large non-reactive bowl with water and squeeze in the juice of a lemon, adding the spent halves as well. This acidulated water will help to prevent the artichokes browning.

Remove the stem at the base, leaving about 2.5 cm (1 in) attached to the artichoke. You can peel the tough outer layer of the stem with a vegetable peeler, if desired. Holding the artichoke firmly in one hand, snap off the tough outer leaves one by one until you reach the more tender, lighter-coloured leaves. Discard the tough leaves.

Next, use a sharp knife to cut 2.5 cm (1 in) off the top of the artichoke, removing the pointy tips of the remaining leaves. Using a teaspoon or a melon baller, scrape out the choke, which is the furry, inedible part at the centre of the artichoke, to reveal the artichoke heart. (This step is typically necessary for larger, mature artichokes; smaller, younger flowers may not have developed a choke.)

Place the trimmed artichoke immediately in the acidulated water to prevent browning, then repeat the process with the remaining artichokes.

Once your artichokes are prepared, you can steam, boil, roast or grill them. Enjoy the delicious artichoke hearts as a standalone dish, served simply dipped into melted butter or added to salads and roasts. One of my favourite ways to enjoy them is with broad beans and lemon, the recipe for which you will find on page 26.

BLACK-EYED PEA SALAD WITH HERBS

The fresh herbs in this salad add flavour and freshness.
I love how the simple act of adding mint to a tomato salad
can give it a refreshing twist, or how adding basil can yield
a sweet and slightly spicy flavour. You can use herbs in
a variety of ways to enhance the taste and texture of many
salads, so don't be afraid to experiment with what you have
on hand.

*

Cook the black-eyed peas in a saucepan of boiling water for
30 minutes or until tender. Drain and rinse under cold running
water, until the peas are cool, then transfer to a large bowl.

Add the tomato, basil, mint, parsley and spring onion to the
black-eyed peas and gently toss to combine.

To make the dressing, whisk the ingredients in a small bowl
until emulsified, then drizzle the dressing over the salad. Gently
toss again to coat the salad in the dressing, then serve.

Serves 4

250 g (9 oz) dried black-eyed peas
2 tomatoes, diced
2 tablespoons chopped basil leaves
2 tablespoons chopped mint leaves
½ small bunch of parsley, leaves picked
    and roughly chopped
1 spring onion (scallion), finely sliced

Honey–lemon dressing

80 ml (⅓ cup) olive oil
zest and juice of 1 lemon
1 teaspoon honey
salt and pepper, to taste

Note   *Black-eyed peas are not only packed with nutrients and
a marvellous nutty flavour, they are also one of the easiest legumes
to prepare as they do not need soaking prior to cooking.*

RAW ZUCCHINI SALAD

This delicate, fresh and easy zucchini salad comes together in minutes and makes a gorgeous summer side dish. Make sure you pick small, tender zucchini, so its gentle flavour can shine through.

✳

Slice the zucchini into long ribbons, using either a mandoline or a very sharp knife, and place in a large bowl. Pour in the olive oil, along with the lemon zest and juice. Season to taste with salt and a generous quantity of pepper, then use your hands to gently mix the ingredients together. Add the basil leaves.

Arrange the zucchini mixture on a serving platter, scatter over the feta and sprinkle with the pine nuts.

Serve immediately as the zucchini will lose its crispness if left for several hours.

Serves 4–6

3 small zucchini (courgettes)
60 ml (¼ cup) olive oil
zest and juice of 1 lemon
salt and pepper, to taste
8 basil leaves, roughly torn
100 g (3½ oz) Greek feta, broken
    into small chunks
1 teaspoon pine nuts (sesame seeds
    are lovely as well)

39

Goes with   *This raw zucchini salad brings a little crunch and freshness when served alongside many of the dishes in this book, but my favourite has to be the Paella on page 86 – it creates the most wonderfully balanced meal.*

ORZO PASTA SALAD

Orzo, also known as risoni, is a small-shaped pasta that looks like rice. In Greek it is known as 'kritharaki', meaning 'barley', and its name perfectly describes its grain-like appearance. I adore orzo and use it often as an alternative to other small pastas in soups, or as a side to rich, tomatoey casseroles as well as salads, such as this one, which is just the thing for a summer lunch or dinner table … a meal on its own or as a side.

❉

Cook the orzo in a saucepan of salted boiling water until al dente, then drain and rinse under cold running water to halt the cooking process. Drain again.

Place the orzo in a large serving bowl, tumble in the tomato, olives, cucumber and red onion, and toss to combine.

In a small bowl, whisk together the olive oil and white balsamic vinegar until emulsified. Season to taste with salt and pepper, then drizzle the dressing over the salad and toss to combine.

Scatter the feta, basil leaves and pine nuts over the top and serve.

Serves 4

250 g (9 oz) orzo (or your favourite
   small-shaped pasta)
500 g (1 lb 2 oz) assorted tomatoes,
   roughly chopped
60 g (2 oz) pitted kalamata olives
1 small cucumber, sliced into rounds
1 small red onion, finely sliced
120 ml (4 fl oz) olive oil
60 ml (¼ cup) white balsamic vinegar
salt and pepper, to taste
125 g (4½ oz) Greek feta, crumbled
½ small bunch of basil, leaves picked
60 g (2 oz) pine nuts, toasted

40

CUCUMBER, WATERMELON & OLIVE SALAD

This is the simplest of summer dishes … refreshing on those hot days when only a light salad will do. The marriage of the ingredients is wonderful – the crispness of the cucumber mingles with the juicy watermelon, while the olives add an unexpected boldness. With each bite I am transported to sun-soaked terraces overlooking the sea.

✽

Place the watermelon, cucumber and olives on a serving platter and toss gently. Top with the chunks of feta and mint leaves and season with black pepper, if desired.

    Serve immediately.

Serves 4

2 kg (4 lb 6 oz) watermelon, rind
   removed, flesh cut into 4 cm
   (1½ in) pieces
1 long cucumber, peeled and cut into
   2 cm (¾ in) pieces
100 g (3½ oz) kalamata olives, pitted
250 g (9 oz) Greek feta, cut into
   large chunks
small bunch of mint, leaves picked
black pepper, to taste (optional)

Goes with   *Serve with the Summer lasagne on page 97 for a sumptuous Sunday lunch or dinner.*

BRAISED TOMATOES
& PEPPERS

The red wine vinegar in this simple dish enhances the
sweetness of the peppers and tomatoes, and I love to
serve it with a generous scattering of parsley, crumbled
feta and olives, and with crusty bread on the side. I find
it's always a good idea to make a double batch and keep
the leftovers in the fridge – they're delicious on a slice
of toast for a quick snack or light lunch; or as a side
to barbecued meats and fish.

*

Heat the olive oil in a large frying pan over medium heat.
Add the red pepper, tomato and garlic, season well and saute for
5–6 minutes, until soft. Reduce the heat to low and continue to
cook until the pepper has collapsed and the tomato has reduced
to a lovely sauce – this could take up to an hour, so keep an eye
on it and stir occasionally, adding a little water if the mixture starts
to dry out. Remove the pan from the heat, stir through the red
wine vinegar and season to taste.

Sprinkle the parsley over the top of the pepper and tomato
mixture, and serve warm or at room temperature, with crusty
bread to mop up the delicious juices and with Greek feta and olives
on the side, if desired.

This dish will keep in an airtight container in the fridge for
2–3 days … if it lasts that long!

Serves 6

100 ml (3½ fl oz) olive oil
12 red peppers (capsicums), chopped
    into 3–4 cm (1¼–1½ in) pieces
6 tomatoes, roughly chopped
3 garlic cloves, finely chopped
salt and pepper, to taste
1 tablespoon red wine vinegar,
    or to taste
parsley leaves, to serve
crusty bread, to serve
Greek feta and olives (optional)

45

Goes with   *This dish is such a staple in my kitchen as it pairs beautifully
with so many of the dishes in this book. Try it with the Zucchini, feta and
mint omelette on page 32 to scoop up all the lovely sauce.*

CAPONATA

One of Sicily's iconic dishes, caponata is made of eggplant, zucchini, tomatoes and sweet and salty olives. The vegetables are lightly sauteed separately to maintain the integrity of their flavour; however, if you prefer, you can bake or grill the vegetables instead. Serve with some crusty bread for a light lunch, as a side dish with grilled meats or chicken, roast potatoes or burrata, or add some croutons to make it a main meal.

❁

Toast the pine nuts in a dry frying pan over medium–low heat, stirring frequently, until golden in colour. Transfer to a small bowl and set aside to cool.

Heat a little of the olive oil in a deep 24 cm (9½ in) frying pan over medium heat. Working in batches and adding more oil as necessary, add the eggplant to the pan and saute for 1–2 minutes, until tender. Transfer to a plate lined with paper towel, then repeat with the zucchini.

Add a little more oil to the pan, along with the onion and celery, and cook for 3–4 minutes, until softened, then add the tomato passata, sugar and red wine vinegar and bring to the boil. Reduce the heat to a simmer and cook for a couple of minutes, until slightly reduced.

Turn the heat off and stir through the cooked eggplant and zucchini, then transfer the mixture to a large bowl and add the tomato, pine nuts, sultanas and olives. Scatter the basil leaves over the vegetables, drizzle with a little extra olive oil and season to taste with salt and pepper, then stir gently and let the vegetables come to room temperature slowly, allowing all the flavours to blend.

Serve with crusty bread.

Serves 4–6

60 g (2 oz) pine nuts
80 ml (⅓ cup) olive oil, plus extra
    for drizzling
1 eggplant (aubergine), cut into 2 cm
    (¾ in) dice
2 zucchini (courgettes), cut into 2 cm
    (¾ in) dice
1 onion, cut into 2 cm (¾ in) dice
3 celery stalks, cut into 2 cm (¾ in) dice
2 tablespoons tomato passata
    (pureed tomatoes)
1 tablespoon caster (superfine) sugar
80 ml (⅓ cup) red wine vinegar
2 tomatoes, cut into 2 cm (¾ in) dice
60 g (½ cup) sultanas (golden raisins)
80 g (2¾ oz) black olives, pitted
small bunch of basil, leaves picked
salt and pepper, to taste
crusty bread, to serve

Make ahead   *This caponata tastes even better the next day, making it the perfect dish to prepare in advance.*

Goes with   *I like to serve this caponata with the Batzina on page 90 or the Zucchini, feta and mint omelette on page 32. It is also wonderful with pasta or spooned onto a slice of crusty bread and topped with some crumbled feta or your favourite cheese.*

ROASTED ZUCCHINI ON LABNEH

Roasted zucchini and labneh make a heavenly marriage, and the sweet and slightly spicy basil is the perfect finishing herb for this springtime salad. If you can't find labneh, you can just as easily use Greek-style yoghurt instead.

❉

Preheat the oven to 200°C (400°F) fan-forced.

Toss the zucchini with the olive oil, then transfer to a baking tray and roast for about 10 minutes, until tender and a little golden around the edges. Remove from the oven and allow to cool.

Place the labneh and lemon zest in a bowl, season with a little salt and pepper and stir to combine. Spoon the labneh onto a serving platter and use the back of a spoon to spread it out.

Arrange the zucchini over the labneh, scatter with the basil leaves and pumpkin seeds and serve.

Serves 4

500 g (1 lb 2 oz) baby zucchini
    (courgettes), sliced into 2 cm
    (¾ in) thick rounds (or lengthways,
    if you prefer)
60 ml (¼ cup) olive oil
200 g (7 oz) labneh
zest of ½ lemon
salt and pepper, to taste
½ small bunch of basil, leaves picked
60 g (2 oz) toasted pumpkin seeds,
    to serve

50

TOMATO & STRAWBERRY SALAD WITH BURRATA

This classic combination of tomatoes and burrata, with the addition of strawberries when they are at their peak, make this salad hard to resist. In addition, the soft flavour of white balsamic vinegar adds a subtle sophistication to the delicate salad dressing. Less intense than regular balsamic vinegar, I also love using it in the orzo salad on page 40 – its floral and fruity notes, with a sweet finish, brighten up many salads.

❋

Whisk together the olive oil and white balsamic vinegar in a small bowl until emulsified, then season to taste with salt and pepper.

Place the strawberry and tomato in a large bowl, drizzle over the dressing and toss well to combine. Spoon the mixture onto a serving platter, leaving room in the centre to place the burrata (if using goat's cheese, you can scatter it over the salad instead).

Garnish the salad with the mint leaves and an extra grinding of black pepper, and serve at room temperature with some crusty bread.

Serves 4

60 ml (¼ cup) olive oil
2 tablespoons white balsamic vinegar
salt and pepper, to taste
200 g (7 oz) strawberries, hulled
    and sliced lengthways
12 small tomatoes, cut into chunks
200 g (7 oz) burrata or soft goat's cheese
½ small bunch of mint, leaves
    roughly torn
crusty bread, to serve

53

Goes with   *Serve this salad alongside the Penne with broccoli, pine nuts and ricotta on page 76 for a match made in heaven.*

POTATO SALAD WITH SAMPHIRE

This is a great salad to bring along to picnics and other outdoor gatherings, as it doesn't contain any foods that will spoil in warmer weather, such as dairy or eggs. Pouring the olive oil onto the potatoes while they are still hot enhances their flavour, as they absorb the oil completely.

You can use sorrel or rocket (arugula) if you can't get your hands on samphire or omit it entirely and use capers instead.

❊

Wash the potatoes well, leaving their skins on, then cut them in half and place in a large saucepan. Cover the potato with cold water, then bring to the boil and cook for 15–20 minutes, until a knife slips through easily.

Meanwhile, wash the samphire gently. Have a taste and if it is too salty for your liking, blanch it in a little hot water for 1 minute, then drain and rinse under cold water and pat dry with paper towel.

Place the samphire, parsley and olives in a serving bowl.

Drain the potato, then return it to the pan and add the olive oil, stirring until the potato absorbs the oil. Add a little more oil if the potato seems dry.

Add the potato to the samphire mixture and toss gently, then season well with salt and pepper. Serve with lemon wedges on the side for squeezing over.

Serves 4

500 g (1 lb 2 oz) small waxy potatoes
100 g (3½ oz) samphire
1 tablespoon parsley leaves
50 g (1¾ oz) kalamata olives, pitted
60 ml (¼ cup) olive oil, plus extra
   if needed
salt and pepper, to taste
lemon wedges, to serve

ROASTED EGGPLANT & TOMATO SALAD

Whether you roast, barbecue or grill eggplant, high-heat cooking will always draw out the vegetable's natural sweetness. The resulting crispy edges and creamy centre are hard to beat, especially in this salad with blistered tomatoes and a zingy yoghurt mixed with salty feta.

*

Preheat the oven to 200°C (400°F) fan-forced. Line one large and one small baking tray with baking paper.

Cut the eggplants into quarters lengthways and place on the large baking tray, cut side up. Drizzle with the olive oil and season well with salt and pepper, then transfer to the oven and roast for 20 minutes, until the eggplant is tender and cooked through.

Meanwhile, place the tomatoes on the small baking tray, drizzle with a little olive oil and roast for 10 minutes, until lightly blistered.

To make the white balsamic vinaigrette, in a small bowl, whisk together the white balsamic vinegar and olive oil until emulsified. Season to taste with salt and pepper, then pour the vinaigrette over the vegetables while they're still warm – this not only helps them absorb the dressing, it also creates a deeper flavour.

Crumble the feta into a bowl, add the yoghurt and stir well, then transfer to a serving platter and spread out using the back of a spoon. Arrange the eggplant and tomatoes on top and scatter over the mint.

Serve straight away.

Serves 4

3 eggplants (aubergines)
60 ml (¼ cup) olive oil, plus extra
    for drizzling
200 g (7 oz) cherry tomatoes on the vine
80 g (2¾ oz) Greek feta
125 g (½ cup) Greek-style yoghurt
2 tablespoons mint leaves

White balsamic vinaigrette

2 tablespoons white balsamic vinegar
3 tablespoons olive oil
salt and pepper, to taste

ZUCCHINI & LENTIL SALAD

Bright-red juicy pomegranates are at their peak in late summer to early autumn. They are a glorious nutrient superhero and utterly delicious, adding a tart sweetness to both savoury and sweet dishes.

This fresh and summery salad, with its assortment of flavours, is delightful served as a light lunch. The combination of nourishing and hearty lentils paired with zucchini, creamy feta and crunchy pistachios and pomegranate seeds is simply wonderful.

❋

Rinse the lentils under cold running water, then add to a large saucepan of boiling water. Cook for about 30 minutes, until the lentils are cooked but not mushy. Drain and rinse again under cold running water to halt the cooking process. Set aside.

Meanwhile, toast the pistachios in a dry frying pan over medium heat until lightly coloured. Transfer to a bowl and allow to cool.

Heat the olive oil in a large frying pan over medium heat. Working in batches, place the zucchini in the pan in a single layer and cook for 3 minutes on each side until golden. Transfer the zucchini to paper towel to drain.

Place the lentils on a serving platter and arrange the zucchini slices over the top.

In a bowl, whisk together the mustard and cumin dressing ingredients until emulsified, then drizzle the dressing over the lentils and zucchini. Crumble the feta over the salad (if using), scatter with the mint leaves, pistachios, pomegranate seeds and lemon zest, and serve.

Serves 4

120 g (4½ oz) green lentils
50 g (1¾ oz) unsalted shelled pistachios
80 ml (⅓ cup) olive oil
2 zucchini (courgettes), finely sliced
100 g (3½ oz) Greek feta (optional)
small handful of mint leaves
1 pomegranate, seeds removed
zest of 1 lemon

Mustard & cumin vinaigrette

100 ml (3½ fl oz) olive oil
3 tablespoons red wine vinegar
½ teaspoon dijon mustard
¼ teaspoon ground cumin
1 teaspoon honey
salt and pepper, to taste

59

How to choose pomegranates   *This jewelled fruit varies naturally in colour from dark pink to medium-to-dark red. No matter the colour, a ripe, sweet and ready-to-eat pomegranate will have a smooth, firm, tough leathery skin, with very few cracks.*

CHARRED COS LETTUCE WITH TAHINI DRESSING

Tahini is full of healthy fats, vitamins and minerals, with a rich, nutty and earthy flavour. It is perhaps best known as an ingredient in hummus, but it is widely used in dishes throughout the Mediterranean. I love it in baba ghanoush or drizzled over Greek-style yoghurt together with some honey for a healthy and delicious breakfast or snack. In a dressing, it makes the perfect accompaniment to charred cos lettuce, or drizzled over a tray of roasted vegetables to make a warm salad.

✳

Using a mortar and pestle, pound the garlic and a little salt until completely crushed. Add the tahini, honey, lemon juice and warm water and mix with the pestle until you have a spoonable dressing. Add pepper to taste and set aside.

Toast the flaked almonds in a dry frying pan over medium–high heat, until golden around the edges. Transfer the flaked almonds to a bowl and set aside.

Wash the lettuce and remove the base of the stalks, then cut each lettuce in half lengthways. Pat dry with paper towel.

Heat a large frying pan over high heat, then reduce the heat a little. Drizzle a little olive oil over the lettuce halves and place in the frying pan, cut side down. Cook for about 3 minutes, until the base of the lettuce is nicely charred, then turn over and cook the other side for another 2 minutes until it is also charred.

Transfer the lettuce to a serving platter and drizzle over the tahini dressing. Scatter with the flaked almonds and serve.

Serves 6

1 garlic clove
salt and pepper, to taste
65 g (¼ cup) hulled tahini
1½ teaspoons honey
juice of 1 lemon
50 ml (1¾ fl oz) warm water
2 tablespoons flaked almonds
3 baby cos (romaine) lettuce
olive oil, for drizzling

Make ahead   *The tahini dressing can be made in advance and stored in a jar in the fridge for up to 3 days.*

Goes with   *The dressing is also lovely spooned over other charred vegetables, or grilled or even raw veg.*

ROASTED BEETROOT & CARROT SALAD WITH LABNEH

The sweetness of roasted beetroot and carrots pairs beautifully with the crunch and slight bitterness of walnuts in this simple but hearty salad. Finished with a light and tangy labneh, and honey–mustard vinaigrette that bring it all together, it's perfect served on its own for a light lunch, or as part of a larger feast alongside roasted or barbecued meats.

✳

To make the labneh, line a colander with a large square of muslin (cheesecloth) and prop it over a bowl, making sure the colander isn't touching the base of the bowl. Spoon the yoghurt into the bowl, followed by the salt and mix gently. Gather the loose corners of the muslin and tie them together (like a money bag) to secure the yoghurt. Transfer to the fridge and leave to drain overnight.

The next day, preheat the oven to 200°C (400°F) fan-forced. Line a large baking tray with baking paper.

Place the beetroot and carrots on the prepared tray and drizzle with enough olive oil to lightly coat the vegetables. Bake for about 45 minutes, until tender, then remove from the oven and place on a plate to cool.

Meanwhile, place the walnuts on a small baking tray and toast in the oven for 4–5 minutes, until golden. Set aside to cool.

To make the honey–mustard vinaigrette, in a small bowl, whisk together the honey, white balsamic vinegar, mustard and olive oil until emulsified. Season to taste with a pinch of salt.

Spoon the labneh onto a serving platter and spread it out using the back of a spoon. Top with the roasted beetroot and carrots and drizzle over the vinaigrette. Scatter the walnuts and dill (if using) over the salad, and serve.

Serves 4

6 small beetroot (beets), scrubbed
 and halved
12 Dutch (baby) carrots, scrubbed
olive oil, for drizzling
50 g (½ cup) walnuts
small bunch of dill, fronds picked
 and chopped (optional)

Labneh

500 g (2 cups) Greek-style yoghurt
1 teaspoon fine sea salt

Honey–mustard vinaigrette

1 tablespoon honey
2 tablespoons white balsamic vinegar
1 teaspoon dijon mustard
60 ml (¼ cup) olive oil
salt, to taste

Note   *The longer you strain the yoghurt, the thicker the labneh will be … overnight is best, about 10 – 12 hours, until it reaches the consistency you enjoy.*

Make ahead   *You can roast the beetroot and carrot the day before and simply bring to room temperature before dressing and serving. Roasted beetroot stores well in an airtight container in the fridge for up to 1 week.*

WATERMELON & FETA SALAD WITH FLAKED ALMONDS, HONEY VINAIGRETTE & MINT

Watermelon and feta are a classic combination that, for me, is summer on a plate. On my last trip to Athens, I ordered a rendition of this salad that was served with pickled watermelon. It was an extra little delight and one that I've emulated here. Serve this salad as an accompaniment to grilled fish or as a light meal on its own.

*

To prepare the pickled watermelon, place the watermelon in a large jar and sprinkle in the sugar. Gently toss the watermelon pieces to coat them in the sugar and allow to sit for 15 minutes. Add the red wine vinegar and mint and allow to sit for a further 20 minutes.

Meanwhile, toast the flaked almonds in a dry frying pan over medium–high heat, until golden around the edges. Transfer to a bowl and set aside.

To make the honey–balsamic vinaigrette, in a small bowl, whisk together the honey, white balsamic vinegar, dijon mustard and olive oil until emulsified, then season to taste with a pinch of salt and pepper.

Place the wedges of watermelon and the feta on a serving platter and scatter the pickled watermelon over the top. Drizzle with the honey–balsamic vinaigrette and garnish with the toasted flaked almonds and mint leaves.

Serves 4

100 g (3½ oz) flaked almonds
600 g (1 lb 5 oz) watermelon, cut into
  thin wedges
250 g (9 oz) Greek feta, broken
  into chunks

65

Pickled watermelon

400 g (14 oz) watermelon, rind removed,
  flesh cut into 2 cm (¾ in) cubes
55 g (¼ cup) caster (superfine) sugar
3 tablespoons red wine vinegar
1 tablespoon chopped mint leaves,
  plus extra leaves to serve

Honey–balsamic vinaigrette

1 teaspoon honey
2 teaspoons white balsamic vinegar
½ teaspoon dijon mustard
3 tablespoons olive oil
salt and pepper, to taste

Goes with   *I like to serve this refreshing watermelon salad alongside the Stuffed tomatoes on page 92.*

GRATING A TOMATO

Watching my mother grate tomatoes to create a luscious tomato puree is a treasured memory. As I close my eyes, I remember my mother wearing her favourite apron, splattered with red juice from the ripe tomatoes, and moving around the kitchen preparing the meal of the day. We would chat, share stories and the kitchen would fill with laughter, forming memories that I hold dear to this day.

During my first trip to Greece, I watched my aunties prepare tomatoes the same way my mother did; it felt like I was witnessing an elegant dance of tradition unfolding before my eyes — the rhythm of their hands moving swiftly, grating the vibrant red tomatoes, took me straight back to my mother's kitchen and our time spent together. I had often asked my mother why she prepared her tomatoes this way. I remember her smiling warmly and explaining that it was what her mother did and her mother before her. My aunties tell me the same when I ask.

Witnessing this simple method in my aunties' homes in Greece, I realised that these culinary rituals are more than just methods of preparing food, they are an expression of love and a way of preserving a culture. Now, whenever I grate tomatoes, I cannot help but feel a connection to my past, to the wisdom passed down among the women in my family and the traditions that have shaped me and my heritage. With each stroke of the grater I feel a sense of belonging, as if I was a part of a timeless tapestry woven together by the love of food and family.

66

One of the most wonderful things about grated tomatoes is how easily you can make a bright, summery sauce. All you need is a box grater, a small knife and a bowl to catch all the wonderful tomatoey flesh and juices.

Slice a small piece off the base of a ripe tomato, creating a flat surface, then hold the other side in the palm of your hand and grate the flat edge against the grater, until all you have left is the skin, which you can discard.

One of my favourite ways to enjoy this tomato puree is to add a little olive oil and a pinch of salt, and spoon some over a slice of toast with a little feta crumbled on top … perfection! And, of course, some of the recipes in this book employ this method too: the Bouyourdi on page 31; Stuffed onion petals (page 81); Arakas (page 75); Spinach fricassee (page 154); Lentil soup (page 139); Paprika roast potatoes (page 166); and Dolmades (page 150).

If you have a glut of ripe summer tomatoes, you can also freeze the tomato puree for up to 6 months, either in freezer bags or a freezer-safe container in portions, ready to add to soups and stews year round.

"The rhythm of their hands moving swiftly, grating the vibrant red tomatoes, took me straight back to my mother's kitchen and our time spent together."

ROASTED EGGPLANT WITH FETA, TOMATO & CARAMELISED ONION

This rustic roasted eggplant is totally delicious. The sweetness of the caramelised onion, one of my favourite ingredients, together with the silky eggplant, tomato and feta is a burst of flavour. Serve it on its own as a complete meal with some crusty bread, on a bed of steamed couscous or as a substantial side to roasted or grilled meats served with a generous spoon of Greek-style yoghurt.

❋

Preheat the oven to 180°C (350°F) fan-forced.

Place the eggplants on a baking tray and roast in the oven for about 1 hour or until softened and cooked through.

Heat the olive oil in a frying pan over low heat and cook the onion, stirring occasionally, for 20–30 minutes, until caramelised. Add the garlic and cook for a further 2 minutes, then transfer the onion mixture to a heatproof bowl and set aside.

Using a small sharp knife, slice the eggplants lengthways and open them up, taking care not to cut them in half completely. Crumble over the feta and top with the tomato, a little salt and pepper, the oregano and caramelised onion. Return to the oven and bake for a further 10–15 minutes, until the feta has melted.

Scatter the basil leaves over the roasted eggplants and serve with crusty bread.

Serves 4–6

3 eggplants (aubergines)
80 ml (⅓ cup) olive oil
2 brown onions, sliced
2 garlic cloves, minced
125 g (4½ oz) Greek feta, crumbled
2 tomatoes, diced
salt and pepper, to taste
1 teaspoon dried oregano
2 tablespoons basil leaves
crusty bread, to serve

ASPARAGUS RISOTTO

The first asparagus of the season heralds the end of winter and the beginning of spring, and I eagerly wait for the first tender spears to appear at the local market. This asparagus risotto is one of my favourite dishes to make in asparagus season. Topped with parmesan, it is a satisfying and elegant meal any time of the week.

❅

Trim the asparagus by snapping off the woody ends, then cut the spears into thirds.

Heat the stock or water in a saucepan over medium heat until simmering, then reduce the heat to low.

Heat the olive oil in a separate saucepan over medium heat and saute the onion for 4–5 minutes, until soft. Add the rice and stir well, so that the rice grains are coated in the oil and onion. Add a ladleful of the hot stock or water to the rice and stir until most of the liquid has been absorbed. Repeat this process, adding the stock or water a ladleful at a time and stirring constantly, for about 15 minutes, until the rice is almost cooked. Add the asparagus and cook, stirring, for a further 5 minutes, then remove from the heat. Stir through the butter, lemon zest and salt and pepper, to taste.

Divide the asparagus risotto among plates, scatter with the grated parmesan and serve.

Serves 4

200 g (7 oz) asparagus spears
1 litre (4 cups) stock or water
3 tablespoons olive oil
1 brown onion, finely diced
250 g (9 oz) arborio rice
50 g (1¾ oz) butter
zest of 1 lemon
salt and pepper, to taste
100 g (3½ oz) parmesan, grated

How to choose asparagus   When selecting asparagus, opt for stalks with a rich green colour, softly fading to white towards the end of the spear. Avoid soft or dull-coloured asparagus, as this indicates they are past their prime.

SPRING — SUMMER

ARAKAS

Lathera is a category of Greek cooking where vegetables are cooked in olive oil, tomatoes and herbs, and this green pea stew is a wonderful example that I love. Served with feta and bread to mop up all the tomatoey sauce, it is a perfect main course or side. The tender fresh spring peas become even sweeter when cooked this way, making them the perfect vegetable in this stew. It is a comforting reminder that spring has arrived.

✻

Heat the olive oil in a large saucepan over medium–high heat, add the onion and saute for 4–5 minutes, until softened. Add the carrot and potato and saute for a further 2 minutes, then add the grated tomato and tomato paste, along with 250 ml (1 cup) of water. Stir well to combine, then add the peas and oregano, and season well with salt and pepper. Bring the mixture to the boil, then reduce the heat to a simmer, cover and cook for 20–30 minutes, until the vegetables are tender and the liquid has thickened.

Serve the green pea stew warm, with a sprinkling of chopped parsley, an extra drizzle of olive oil, chunks of feta and crusty bread.

Serves 4

80 ml (⅓ cup) olive oil, plus extra
    for drizzling
1 brown onion, finely diced
3 carrots, diced
2 potatoes, cut into chunks
3 tomatoes, grated
1 tablespoon tomato paste
    (concentrated puree)
500 g (1 lb 2 oz) freshly podded peas
1 teaspoon dried oregano
salt and pepper, to taste

To serve

1 tablespoon chopped parsley leaves
Greek feta
crusty bread

75

PENNE WITH BROCCOLI, PINE NUTS & RICOTTA

I have used penne for this dish, but orecchiette would also be wonderful. To maintain the vibrant green colour of the broccoli, be sure to rinse it under cold water once it's cooked. Closely related to cabbage, brussels sprouts, kale and cauliflower, broccoli is nutritious and delicious raw, roasted, steamed or boiled.

❁

Cook the pasta in a large saucepan of salted boiling water until al dente.

Meanwhile, bring another saucepan of water to the boil, add the broccoli and cook for just a few minutes, until tender but still with a light crunch. Drain and rinse the broccoli under cold running water to halt the cooking process and maintain its colour, then set aside.

Heat the olive oil in a large frying pan over medium heat, add the garlic and saute for 4–5 minutes, until softened. Add the pine nuts and saute for a further 2 minutes, then add the broccoli and stir to combine well.

Drain the pasta and add it to the broccoli mixture, tossing well to combine. Season to taste with salt and pepper, then stir through the ricotta.

Divide the pasta among shallow bowls, sprinkle with grated parmesan or pecorino, a few chilli flakes and a little lemon zest (if using), and serve.

Serves 4

400 g (14 oz) penne
400 g (14 oz) broccoli,
    broken into florets
3 tablespoons olive oil
1 garlic clove, minced
60 g (2 oz) pine nuts
salt and pepper, to taste
120 g (4½ oz) ricotta

To serve

grated parmesan or pecorino
chilli flakes (optional)
lemon zest (optional)

Goes with   *The Tomato & strawberry salad with burrata on page 53 goes beautifully with this dish. The dreamy burrata, made of mozzarella and cream, along with the ricotta in this pasta, makes everything extra indulgent.*

FASOLAKIA

Fasolakia, a traditional bean stew, is such a simple yet flavoursome Mediterranean dish, and one of my go-to meals in midsummer. If I have a glut of green beans, in addition to making this stew, I like to lightly grill them and dress simply with olive oil, a squeeze of lemon and a sprinkling of salt – it is an absolutely delicious way to enjoy them.

✿

Heat the olive oil in a large saucepan over medium heat, add the onion and saute for 3–4 minutes, until soft. Add the garlic and saute for another couple of minutes, then add the tomatoes, oregano and cinnamon. Season well with salt and pepper, then bring the mixture to a simmer and cook for 4–5 minutes, until the tomatoes have reduced slightly. Add 250 ml (1 cup) of water and stir to combine.

Add the beans, zucchini, carrot and potato (if using) to the pan, bring the mixture to the boil, then reduce the heat to a simmer. Cover with a lid and cook for 15–20 minutes, adding a little more water if the mixture starts to look dry, until the vegetables are tender and cooked through.

Sprinkle with the chopped parsley (if using) and serve the fasolakia warm, with crusty bread to mop up all the delicious juices and chunks of salty feta.

Serves 4

60 ml (¼ cup) olive oil
1 brown onion, diced
2 garlic cloves, finely chopped
1 × 400 g (14 oz) tin chopped tomatoes
½ teaspoon dried oregano
pinch of ground cinnamon
salt and pepper, to taste
600 g (1 lb 5 oz) green beans, trimmed
    if necessary
1 zucchini (courgette), sliced into rounds
2 carrots, sliced into rounds
1 potato, chopped into small chunks
    (optional)
2 tablespoons chopped parsley leaves
    (optional)
crusty bread, to serve
Greek feta, to serve

Freezing beans   *Green beans freeze incredibly well – simply wash and pat dry, then trim and place in zip-lock bags in the freezer. You'll have sweet-from-the-summer-sun beans for months to come.*

STUFFED ONION PETALS

Onion petals stuffed with rice and tomatoes is a dish
I first ate in Thessaloniki, Greece, and many variations
of this simple and nourishing meal can be found throughout
the region and surrounding islands. Here, I have added
pine nuts, sultanas and one of my favourite spices, sweet
paprika. These delicate morsels take a little time to prepare,
but the results are absolutely worth it.

*

Preheat the oven to 180°C (350°F) fan-forced.

Using a small sharp knife, trim the tops of the red onions,
then slice down the middle on one side, from the top to the bottom,
leaving the base intact.

Bring a saucepan of water to the boil, carefully lower in the
onions, then reduce the heat to a simmer and cook for about
10 minutes, until the onions are tender. Drain and set aside to cool.

Heat the olive oil in a frying pan over medium heat and saute
the diced onion for 4–5 minutes, until soft. Add the rice, grated
tomato, parsley, pine nuts, sultanas and paprika, season well with
salt and pepper and simmer for 5–6 minutes, until reduced slightly
and the rice is par-cooked. Remove from the heat and allow to cool.

Carefully peel the petal layers from the cooled red onions.
Place an onion petal in the palm of your hand, top with a tablespoon
of the rice mixture and roll it up using the other hand (I like to hold
the onion petal as it gives me more control over the rolling).
Lay the stuffed onion petal in a baking dish, packed tightly so
it doesn't unroll, then continue with the remaining onion and rice
mixture, filling the dish as you go. Drizzle a little extra olive oil
over the stuffed petals and pour in 250 ml (1 cup) of water.
Place an ovenproof plate on top so the stuffed petals stay in place,
then transfer to the oven and bake for 30 minutes or until the
rice is cooked through.

Serve the stuffed onion petals with a squeeze of lemon juice
and some crusty bread.

Serves 4

6 red onions, peeled
80 ml (⅓ cup) olive oil, plus extra
    for drizzling
1 brown onion, finely diced
120 g (4½ oz) medium-grain rice
4 large tomatoes, grated
2 tablespoons finely chopped
    parsley leaves
100 g (⅔ cup) pine nuts, toasted
100 g (3½ oz) sultanas (golden raisins)
½ teaspoon sweet paprika
salt and pepper, to taste
lemon wedges, to serve
crusty bread, to serve

81

PUMPKIN & FETA PIE

With the earthy sweetness of pumpkin, spices and plump currants all wrapped in golden, crunchy, flaky pastry, I could eat this scrumptious filo pie at any time of the day. Don't be tempted to skip the drizzle of honey at the end – it complements the buttery pastry and savoury filling fabulously. Alternatively, you can serve it with Greek-style yoghurt.

*

Preheat the oven to 200°C (400°F) fan-forced.

Place the pumpkin on a large baking tray in a single layer. Drizzle with a little olive oil and bake for 20–25 minutes, until soft and golden around the edges. Remove the pumpkin from the oven and allow to cool.

Place the pumpkin in a bowl and smash the pieces using a fork. Add the cinnamon, nutmeg, currants, feta, eggs and mint. Season well with salt and pepper and stir to combine the ingredients.

Melt the butter in a small saucepan over medium heat. Remove from the heat and add the olive oil. Brush a 24 cm (9½ in) round baking tin or dish with a little of the butter and oil mixture.

Lay out a sheet of the filo pastry with a long edge facing you and brush with some of the butter and oil. Scatter 3–4 tablespoons of the pumpkin mixture over the filo pastry, then, starting with the edge of the pastry closest to you, concertina the filo into a long strip, then coil it in on itself to create a spiral. Place the coil in the centre of the baking tin, then continue with the remaining pastry, most of the butter and oil mixture and all of the filling, adding the concertinaed strips to the central spiral, until you have a large spiral-shaped pie.

Brush the pie with the remaining butter and oil, sprinkle with a little water and bake for 30–40 minutes, until crisp and golden brown.

Serve warm with a drizzle of honey.

Serves 6–8

800 g (1 lb 12 oz) pumpkin (winter squash), cut into 2 cm (¾ in) pieces
125 ml (½ cup) olive oil, plus extra for drizzling
1 teaspoon ground cinnamon
¼ teaspoon freshly grated nutmeg
60 g (2 oz) currants
100 g (3½ oz) Greek feta, crumbled
3 eggs
2 tablespoons finely chopped mint leaves
salt and pepper, to taste
50 g (1¾ oz) butter
250 g (9 oz) store-bought refrigerated filo pastry
honey, to serve

82

SUMMER PAELLA

Situated on the east coast of Spain, Valencia is undeniably the home of paella, one of the Mediterranean's most celebrated dishes, with its many variations. I do love a one-pan meal and this iconic rice dish is equally at home serving a crowd or small family gathering. I encourage you to embellish this recipe with your choice of seafood (squid and prawns are great), poultry or chorizo, or other vegetables you have on hand.

*

Preheat the oven to 200°C (400°F) fan-forced.

Place the red peppers on a baking tray and roast, turning occasionally, for 30 minutes or until they are blackened. Remove the peppers from the oven and set aside until cool enough to handle, then peel and remove the seeds and tear the flesh into strips.

Heat a large paella pan or wide-based frying pan over medium heat and add the olive oil. Add the onion, green beans and green pepper and saute for 2–3 minutes, until soft. Add the garlic, smoked paprika, chopped tomatoes and three-quarters of the vegetable stock or water. Bring to the boil, then reduce the heat to a simmer.

Meanwhile, infuse the saffron threads in 60 ml (¼ cup) of water for a few minutes, then pour into the paella pan and stir to combine. Season with salt and pepper.

Add the rice and roasted red pepper strips to the pan and stir to coat the rice in the tomatoey vegetable sauce. Shake the pan gently from side to side to settle the rice in an even layer, then cook, stirring occasionally and adding the remaining stock or water as the rice absorbs the liquid, for about 15 minutes, until the rice is al dente. The base of the rice should develop a crispy, caramelised crust as it cooks – in Spain, this is known as the socarrat and it's the most-prized part of the paella.

Serve the paella in the pan with a generous amount of parsley and lemon wedges on the side for squeezing over.

Serves 4

3 red peppers (capsicums)
2 tablespoons olive oil
1 brown onion, diced
200 g (7 oz) green beans, trimmed and
    sliced into quarters on an angle
1 green pepper (capsicum),
    cut into chunks
4 garlic cloves, finely chopped
1 teaspoon smoked paprika
1 × 400 g (14 oz) tin chopped tomatoes
1 litre (4 cups) vegetable stock or water
pinch of saffron threads
salt and pepper, to taste
300 g (10½ oz) paella rice,
    such as bomba or calasparra
small bunch of parsley, leaves picked
lemon wedges, to serve

Goes with   *The Charred cos lettuce with tahini dressing on page 60 makes an excellent side salad to this light-tasting paella.*

ROAST TOMATO TART

Roasting in-season tomatoes enhances their sweetness, which provides a wonderful contrast to the saltiness of the olives in this summer tomato tart. The flaky pastry is so versatile and works equally well in savoury and sweet tarts and galettes – try it in other recipes that call for pastry and I promise that you won't be disappointed.

Serve this tart with chunks of feta at your next summer picnic – I guarantee everyone will love it.

❊

Heat the olive oil in a large frying pan over medium heat. Add the onion and saute for 5–6 minutes, until softened and slightly caramelised – I like to add a splash of water while the onion cooks so it doesn't burn. Remove from the heat and set aside to cool.

Preheat the oven to 180°C (350°F) fan-forced. Line a large baking tray with baking paper.

Roll the dough out on a lightly floured work surface to a 30 cm (12 in) circle, about 3 cm (1¼ in) thick, then transfer to the prepared tray. Spread the cooled caramelised onion over the base of the pastry, leaving a 3–4 cm (1¼–1½ in) border. Dot with the kalamata olives and arrange the tomato slices, overlapping, over the top. Season with black pepper.

Fold the pastry border over the outside edge of the filling, pinching the pastry as you go to secure. Brush the pastry with the beaten egg.

Bake the tart for about 40 minutes or until the pastry is golden. Serve at room temperature.

Serves 4

60 ml (¼ cup) olive oil
2 brown onions, finely sliced
1 × quantity Flaky pastry (see page 114)
plain (all-purpose) flour, for dusting
80 g (2¾ oz) kalamata olives, pitted
   and halved
6 tomatoes, sliced 5 mm (¼ in) thick
black pepper
1 egg, lightly beaten

Make ahead   *The pastry can be made up to 2 days in advance. Wrap well and keep in the fridge.*

BATZINA

Crustless zucchini pie

Batzina is a crustless zucchini pie from the region of Thessaly in Central Greece, where it was traditionally made as a thin slice to enable quick cooking and for it to stay crisp for more than a few hours. It was a meal that farmers could easily take with them to the fields and children could take to school. It makes a perfect summer's day dish, and even breakfast, when zucchini is in abundance and at its best. It's delicious served with olives and pickles!

❉

Preheat the oven to 180°C (350°F) fan-forced. Lightly grease a 25 × 35 cm (10 × 13¾ in) baking dish with oil.

Grate the zucchini using the large holes of a box grater. Transfer to a large bowl, sprinkle over a little salt, then use your hands to massage the zucchini and squeeze out any excess moisture. Set aside for 15 minutes.

Place the zucchini in a clean tea towel and squeeze out the extra water, then transfer to a clean bowl. Stir through the herbs, then add the eggs, feta, yoghurt, lemon zest and olive oil, season to taste with salt and pepper and mix well to combine.

In a separate bowl, combine the flour and baking powder, then add this to the zucchini mixture and mix well until no bits of flour remain. Pour the mixture into the prepared dish and use the back of a spoon to smooth the surface. Transfer to the oven and bake the batzina for 40–45 minutes, until golden around the edges and set in the middle.

Allow the batzina to cool, then cut into slices and serve warm or at room temperature. Any leftovers will keep in an airtight container in the fridge for 2–3 days.

Serves 6

1 kg (2 lb 3 oz) zucchini (courgettes), trimmed
salt and pepper, to taste
2 tablespoons finely chopped mint leaves
2 tablespoons finely chopped basil leaves
1 tablespoon finely chopped dill fronds
3 eggs
350 g (12½ oz) Greek feta, crumbled
250 g (1 cup) Greek-style yoghurt
zest of 1 lemon
3 tablespoons olive oil
125 g (4½ oz) plain (all-purpose) flour
1 teaspoon baking powder

Goes with   *Serve with a side of Caponata (see page 46) for a wonderful lunch option.*

STUFFED TOMATOES

Baking trays filled with stuffed tomatoes remind me of warm days spent in the Med. In this recipe, I combine the sweetness of summer's best tomatoes, bursting with flavour, with the nuttiness of farro, and its hint of cinnamon, as well as fragrant herbs. Served with refreshing yoghurt, it is a dish I know you will love.

Season the tomatoes and potatoes well before baking and use the best-quality olive oil you can.

*

Preheat the oven to 180°C (350°F) fan-forced.

Cut the tops off the tomatoes and set aside. Use a teaspoon to scoop out most of the tomato flesh, leaving a 1 cm (½ in) border and taking care to not pierce the skin. Chop the flesh finely and place in a bowl. Arrange the tomato shells in a large baking dish.

Heat the olive oil in a large frying pan over medium heat. Add the onion and saute for 4–5 minutes, until softened. Add the rice and farro and stir well to combine, then pour in the tomato flesh and 250 ml (1 cup) of water. Bring the mixture to a simmer and cook for about 10 minutes, until the rice and farro are slightly softened. Add the pine nuts, raisins, dill, mint and parsley, then reduce the heat to low and cook for a further 2 minutes. Remove the pan from the heat and season the mixture well with salt and pepper.

Stuff the tomatoes with the rice mixture almost to the top, allowing room for the filling to expand, and cover with the tops. Place the potato wedges among the tomatoes and spoon any leftover filling into any gaps in the dish. Season the potatoes, then pour 125 ml (½ cup) of water into the dish, along with a generous drizzle of olive oil. Bake for 1 hour, or until the filling is tender and the potato wedges are cooked.

Serve with yoghurt on the side.

Serves 4–6

12 tomatoes
60 ml (¼ cup) olive oil, plus extra
    for drizzling
1 brown onion, finely diced
330 g (1½ cups) short-grain rice
110 g (4 oz) farro
40 g (¼ cup) pine nuts
60 g (½ cup) raisins
2 tablespoons finely chopped dill fronds
3 tablespoons finely chopped mint leaves
3 tablespoons finely chopped parsley leaves
salt and pepper, to taste
3 potatoes, peeled and cut into wedges
Greek-style yoghurt, to serve

Goes with *The Watermelon & feta salad with flaked almonds, honey vinaigrette & mint on page 65 adds a delightful freshness when served with this dish as part of a spread.*

BAKED OKRA & TOMATO

Throughout Greece, okra is traditionally served as a stew with chicken and, in some regions, with fish. It has a mild, almost grassy, flavour that is quite unique and can be best described as a combination of eggplant (aubergine) and asparagus. If you are using fresh okra, keep them whole to reduce the vegetable's mucilaginous texture, which some people find off-putting. Frozen okra is a great alternative.

❋

To prepare fresh okra, trim the stems with a small sharp knife, taking care not to pierce the flesh. Transfer to a non-reactive bowl and gently swish the white wine vinegar over the okra to coat. Set aside for 30 minutes, then drain and rinse well. If you are using tinned or frozen okra you can skip this step.

Preheat the oven to 180°C (350°F) fan-forced.

Heat the olive oil in a frying pan over medium heat. Add the onion and saute for 4–5 minutes, until soft, then add the garlic and cook for a further 2–3 minutes. Add the chopped tomatoes and 375 ml (1½ cups) of water and simmer for 4–5 minutes, until slightly reduced. Stir through the parsley and oregano and season well, to taste, then add the okra and stir gently to combine.

Transfer the okra and tomato mixture to a 24 cm (9½ in) round baking dish and lay the peppers, skin side up, over the top. Transfer to the oven and bake for about 1 hour, until the okra is soft and the sauce has thickened. Stir the mixture occasionally and keep an eye on the sauce as it cooks, adding a little water if it starts to look dry. Remove from the oven and add a squeeze of lemon and a scattering of extra parsley, if desired.

Serve, perhaps with some crusty bread, feta and a green salad.

Serves 4

500 g (1 lb 2 oz) fresh, tinned
   or frozen okra
125 ml (½ cup) white wine vinegar
   (if using fresh okra)
60 ml (¼ cup) olive oil
1 brown onion, chopped
2 garlic cloves, finely chopped
1 × 400 g (14 oz) tin chopped tomatoes
2 tablespoons chopped parsley,
   plus extra leaves to serve (optional)
1 teaspoon dried oregano
salt and pepper, to taste
2 long green or red peppers
   (capsicums), halved lengthways
squeeze of lemon juice, to serve

95

Choosing okra *Also known as ladies' fingers, okra is a vegetable that often evokes a strong reaction: you either love it or hate it. If you can get past their slightly slimy texture, I promise you that their flavour is subtle and delicious. To select okra, look for small, slim pods with no bulging middle. They should also be firm to touch, indicating that the okra is fresh. Okra does not keep well – I recommend storing the pods in an airtight container in the fridge and consuming within 2–3 days.*

SUMMER LASAGNE

Lasagne is one of my favourite comfort foods and this version, with late summer zucchini and butternut pumpkin, light ricotta and creamy bechamel, is soothing and super delicious. There are no limits to what vegetables you can include in this lasagne, so add what's in season and make it your own.

*

Preheat the oven to 180°C (350°F) fan-forced. Line a large baking tray with baking paper.

Place the pumpkin on the prepared tray, brush both sides with a little olive oil and season with salt and pepper. Transfer to the oven and roast for 15 minutes or until almost tender. Set aside.

Heat a couple of tablespoons of olive oil in a large frying pan over medium heat. Add the zucchini and fry gently for 3–4 minutes on both sides, until golden (you may need to do this in batches). Season, then remove from the pan and set aside.

To make the tomato sauce, heat the olive oil in a large saucepan over medium heat. Add the onion, garlic, celery and carrot and saute for 5 minutes, then add the tomatoes, wine, bay leaves, oregano, basil and 250 ml (1 cup) of water. Season well and simmer for 15 minutes or until reduced slightly.

To make the bechamel, melt the butter in a large saucepan over medium heat. Add the flour and stir using a wooden spoon for a couple of minutes until the mixture is slightly golden. Add the milk, a little at a time and stirring constantly to avoid lumps forming, until completely incorporated. Add a generous amount of grated nutmeg and season well with salt and pepper. Continue to cook the bechamel, stirring as you cook, for about 10 minutes, until thickened and smooth. Remove the pan from the heat and add the egg, mixing well to combine.

To assemble the lasagne, spread one-third of the tomato sauce over the base of a 25 × 35 cm (10 × 13¾ in) baking dish and top with one-third of the lasagne sheets. Add one-third of the roasted pumpkin, followed by one-third of the zucchini, then dollop one-third of the ricotta over the vegetables and sprinkle with a third of the Parmigiano Reggiano. Finally, drizzle over one-third of the bechamel. Repeat the layers twice more, finishing with a layer of bechamel.

Transfer the lasagne to the oven and bake for about 30 minutes, until golden and bubbling.

Serve the lasagne with a simple green salad or the suggestion below.

Goes with   *Serve this lasagne with the Cucumber, watermelon & olive salad on page 42, along with some crusty bread and a glass of fruity rose.*

Serves 6

800 g (1 lb 12 oz) butternut pumpkin (squash), peeled and cut into 1 cm (½ in) thick slices
olive oil
salt and pepper, to taste
3 zucchini (courgettes), sliced into 1 cm (½ in) thick rounds
250 g (9 oz) fresh lasagne sheets
60 g (2 oz) Parmigiano Reggiano, grated
375 g (1½ cups) ricotta

Tomato sauce

60 ml (¼ cup) olive oil
1 brown onion, finely diced
2 garlic cloves, roughly chopped
2 celery stalks, finely diced
1 carrot, finely diced
2 × 400 g (14 oz) tins whole tomatoes
60 ml (¼ cup) red wine
2 dried bay leaves
½ teaspoon dried oregano
12 basil leaves, roughly torn
salt and pepper, to taste

Bechamel

100 g (3½ oz) butter
80 g (2¾ oz) plain (all-purpose) flour
1 litre (4 cups) full-cream (whole) milk
freshly grated nutmeg
1 egg

97

I remember fondly the days when I would help my mother in the kitchen at pickling time. Our favourite was always stuffed peppers but I genuinely loved them all.

Pickled vegetables aren't only an explosion of flavour to serve alongside other dishes, such as grilled meats, soups and stews, or in a salad or sandwich, they also make the perfect meze plate with cheese and bread. When eaten with beans and other legumes, pickles aid digestion.

There is something comforting about having jars of pickles in your pantry, and the recipes that follow are on rotation and are staples in my kitchen year-round. They are easy to prepare and you don't need to be an expert pickler to make them.

Pickling is such a great way to use up leftover vegetables or when they are in abundance … simply cut to size, add aromatic spices that you love, cover in brine, seal and wait for magic to happen. There are also no rules when it comes to selecting jars – simply choose vessels that suit the size and shape of the veg you are pickling … tall jars for eggplants (aubergines), large round jars for peppers (capsicums) etc..

For most pickles, you should ideally wait at least 2 weeks before opening the jar and transferring to the fridge, but waiting another week will allow the veg to further mellow and develop an even deeper flavour. The exception to this is my recipe for pickled cucumbers, which can be consumed the next day.

99

PICKLED EGGPLANT

Cut the eggplants into quarters lengthways, sprinkle with a little salt and set aside in a colander for 30 minutes. Rinse the eggplant and gently squeeze out any excess liquid.

Select a few tall jars (to better accommodate the eggplant spears), then sterilise your jars and lids following the instructions on page 21.

Place the white wine vinegar, sugar, 1 teaspoon of salt, the peppercorns, garlic, oregano, chilli flakes and 190 ml (6½ fl oz) of water in a large saucepan and bring to the boil. Reduce the heat to a simmer and cook for 6 minutes.

Divide the eggplant among the sterilised jars so that each jar is three-quarters full. Pour the hot pickling liquid over the eggplant to cover completely, then finish with the olive oil. Seal the jars and allow to cool.

Store the jars in a cool, dark place – they will be ready to eat after a couple of weeks. Unopened, the pickled eggplant will keep for up to 1 year. Once opened, transfer to the fridge and consume within 2 months.

Makes 1 kg (2 lb 3 oz)

1 kg (2 lb 3 oz) medium eggplants
  (aubergines)
salt
375 ml (1½ cups) white wine vinegar
50 g (1¾ oz) sugar
½ teaspoon black peppercorns
2 garlic cloves, minced
1 teaspoon dried oregano
¼ teaspoon chilli flakes
3 tablespoons olive oil

100

A WELL-TRAVELLED FRUIT

The eggplant, or aubergine, has a reputation of sparking debates: to salt or not to salt before cooking. Thankfully, many of the bitter qualities in common eggplant varieties have been bred out over time. Personally, I don't find it necessary to salt my eggplant, and I believe the same for you.

Eggplants were first domesticated in what is now modern-day India and China, with wild species first growing in northeastern Africa more than two million years ago and then spreading east towards Asia. Over centuries of trade and cultural exchanges, traders and travellers introduced eggplants to the Mediterranean, highlighting the interconnectedness of cultures and the lasting impact of culinary exchanges throughout history. The eggplant soon became an integral part of the Mediterranean cuisine, mainly due to its versatility and ability to absorb flavours from various ingredients, herbs and spices.

Today, there are several varieties of eggplants, each with their own unique character. The most common is the large globe eggplant, with its dark purple, smooth, glossy skin and creamy, mild flesh that makes it a great choice for most recipes. Then there's the Italian eggplant, which is similar to the globe but generally smaller in size, with a teardrop shape and a slightly sweeter taste. It is ideal for grilling, frying and braising – see my recipe for Caponata on page 46 – or roasting and pairing with beans, such as my Roasted eggplant with cannellini beans on page 196.

Sicilian eggplants are small and round, with a light pink or lavender skin and a custard-like sweet flesh. I encourage you to buy some if you spot them at your local farmers' market and make my Pickled stuffed eggplants on page 104. Graffiti eggplants have a purple-and-white-striped skin that's thinner than other varieties, with smaller seeds and a sweet taste. While still considered an Italian eggplant, it is larger than the Sicilian cultivar and perfect roasted whole, then split open and drizzled with your favourite dressing or topping.

"The most delightful eggplant dishes often involve grilling, roasting or frying with ample use of fats."

103

Chinese eggplants are long and thin with a pastel-purple-lilac colour and similar taste to the Japanese eggplant, which has a deeper purple skin. They are both wonderful fried and pickled. Finally, the Indian eggplant is often referred to as baby eggplant as it is one of the smallest varieties. Plump and round with a rich purple skin, it is ideal for stuffing and roasting.

The most delightful eggplant dishes often involve grilling, roasting or frying with ample use of fats. Eggplants act like large sponges, and they truly shine when generously coated with luscious olive oil. No matter how you prepare them, it may appear as if you are using an abundant amount of oil, but this 'extravagance' is essential to unlocking the full potential of their exquisite flavour.

Different regions around the Mediterranean have their own way of preparing eggplant dishes. In Italy, the eggplant is a staple in pasta dishes, as well as one of my all-time favourites, Caponata. In Greece, the classic moussaka is revered, while over in Turkey the famous imam bayildi is a much-celebrated dish, once enjoyed only by sultans.

When choosing eggplants, select ones that are firm, heavy for their size and free from blemishes.

PICKLED STUFFED EGGPLANTS

Trim the stalks from the eggplants and use a small sharp knife to insert three slits into the eggplants lengthways.

Place the eggplants in a large saucepan, add 200 ml (7 fl oz) of water and bring to the boil. Add the white wine vinegar, salt and sugar, then reduce the heat to a simmer and cook for about 4 minutes, until the eggplants are soft. Remove the eggplants from the pickling liquid using a slotted spoon and rinse well under cold water.

Blanch the celery stalks in the hot pickling liquid for a couple of minutes, then remove and cut into long thin strips.

Sterilise your jars and lids following the instructions on page 21.

Combine the grated carrot, garlic, parsley and chilli flakes (if using) in a bowl. Holding an eggplant in the palm of one hand, use the other hand to stuff the slits with the carrot mixture. Carefully place the stuffed eggplant on your work surface and wrap a strip of celery around the eggplant. Tie the celery in a knot to hold the eggplant together and secure the filling. Repeat with the remaining eggplants, filling and celery, then transfer the stuffed eggplants to the prepared jars and pour the pickling liquid over the top to cover completely. Finish with the peppercorns and olive oil, then seal the jars and allow to cool.

Store the jars in a cool, dark place for 2 weeks before eating. Unopened jars will keep for up to 1 year. Refrigerate once opened and consume within 2 months.

These eggplants are so beautiful and once stuffed, secured with the celery strip and pickled, they will be a star in your kitchen.

104

Makes 600 g (1 lb 5 oz)

500 g (1 lb 2 oz) small Sicilian
   eggplants (aubergines)
250 ml (1 cup) white wine vinegar
1 teaspoon salt
50 g (1¾ oz) sugar
2 celery stalks
2 carrots, grated
2 garlic cloves, minced
2 tablespoons chopped parsley leaves
¼ teaspoon chilli flakes (optional)
½ teaspoon black peppercorns
3 tablespoons olive oil

PICKLED CUCUMBERS

Sterilise a large jar and lid following the instructions on page 21.

Cut the cucumbers into halves lengthways and place in the sterilised jar.

Combine the white wine vinegar, olive oil, garlic, sugar, bay leaves, peppercorns, salt, dill seeds and 250 ml (1 cup) of water in a saucepan and bring to the boil. Reduce the heat to a simmer and cook for 8 minutes, then remove from the heat and allow to cool.

Pour the cooled pickling brine into the jar, covering the cucumber completely. Seal and give the jar a couple of taps on a work surface to release any air bubbles.

Refrigerate overnight and enjoy the next day. The pickled cucumbers will keep in the fridge for up to 2 months.

Makes 500 g (1 lb 2 oz)

500 g (1 lb 2 oz) small pickling cucumbers

500 ml (2 cups) white wine vinegar

60 ml (¼ cup) olive oil

2 garlic cloves, finely diced

60 g (2 oz) sugar

2 bay leaves

12 black peppercorns

1 tablespoon salt

1 teaspoon dill seeds

109

PICKLED STUFFED PEPPERS

Combine the shredded cabbage, grated carrot and parsley in a bowl.

Remove the stems from the peppers and carefully scrape out the seeds and membranes. Turn the peppers over and score the base with a small sharp knife, then fill the peppers with the cabbage mixture.

Sterilise one large or two smaller jars and lids following the instructions on page 21. Add the stuffed peppers to the jar/s.

Place the white wine vinegar, salt, sugar, peppercorns, bay leaf, minced garlic and 500 ml (2 cups) of water in a saucepan and bring to the boil. Reduce the heat to a simmer and cook for 3 minutes, whisking well to dissolve the salt and sugar completely.

Pour the hot pickling liquid over the peppers, making sure they are submerged, then finish with the olive oil and seal with the lid/s.

Store the jars in a cool, dark place – they will be ready to eat after 2–3 weeks. Unopened, the pickled peppers will keep for up to 1 year. Once opened, transfer to the fridge and consume within 2 months.

Makes 1 kg (2 lb 3 oz)

300 g (10½ oz) white cabbage, finely shredded
100 g (3½ oz) carrots, grated
¼ bunch of parsley, leaves picked and finely chopped
500 g (1 lb 2 oz) small red peppers (capsicums)
250 ml (1 cup) white wine vinegar
1 tablespoon salt
250 g (9 oz) caster (superfine) sugar
½ teaspoon black peppercorns
1 bay leaf
2 garlic cloves, minced
60 ml (¼ cup) olive oil

110

APRICOT TART

Apricots make a wonderful filling for a tart. Once you are comfortable with this recipe, try swapping the fruit for other stone fruit, such as peaches, nectarines, plums and cherries, or in autumn and winter, using apples or pears, or a combination, with a sprinkling of ground cinnamon.

The flaky pastry is perfect for all sorts of sweet and savoury tarts and galettes. The key is to make sure that the water and butter are very cold before making the dough.

❊

To make the flaky pastry, place the flour, sugar and salt in a large bowl and stir gently to combine. Add the butter and use your fingertips to rub the butter into the flour, until you have small, flat pieces of butter, which is what you want rather than it resembling breadcrumbs. Drizzle in the apple cider vinegar and slowly add the water, mixing as you go, until the dough comes together into a ball. Flatten the ball a little, then wrap in plastic wrap and chill in the fridge for 1 hour.

Meanwhile, combine the almond meal and sugar in a large bowl, add the cream and mix well. Add the egg and stir through.

Take the pastry out of the fridge and allow it to come back to room temperature for 10–15 minutes.

On a lightly floured work surface, roll out the pastry into a 22 cm (8¾ in) circle and transfer to a baking tray lined with baking paper. Spread the almond cream over the pastry, leaving a 3 cm border around the edge. Place the apricot halves on top, cut side up, then fold the pastry border over the outside edge of the filling, pinching the pastry as you go to secure.

Brush the pastry with extra cream and sprinkle demerara sugar all over the tart, then place in the fridge to chill for 30 minutes.

Meanwhile, preheat the oven to 200°C (400°F) fan-forced.

Bake the tart for 30–35 minutes, until the pastry is golden and the apricot is soft.

Allow the tart to cool before serving. It is delicious with a scoop of vanilla ice cream or a dollop of cream.

Serves 6

100 g (1 cup) almond meal
1 tablespoon sugar
2 tablespoons pure cream, plus extra
    for brushing
1 egg
8 apricots, halved, stones removed
demerara sugar, for sprinkling

Flaky pastry

170 g (6 oz) plain (all-purpose) flour,
    plus extra for dusting
1 teaspoon caster (superfine) sugar
pinch of salt
100 g (3½ oz) cold butter, cut into cubes
1 tablespoon apple cider vinegar
80 ml (⅓ cup) iced water

114

Choosing apricots *In a perfect world, apricots are best picked ripe from the tree, but as we don't all have apricot trees in our gardens, look for plump fruit with a deep-orange or gold colour, and just a tiny softness to them.*

CHERRY CLAFOUTIS

This clafoutis is so easy – simply whisk together the ingredients for the batter, pour into a baking dish over the cherries and bake in the oven. Traditionally, the French cherry clafoutis contains fruit with the pits, but I have removed them for this recipe, as it makes for a more enjoyable eating experience. This dessert is a wonderful way to use cherries when they're in peak season.

❈

Preheat the oven to 180°C (350°F) fan-forced.

Lightly grease a 24 cm (9½ in) round baking dish and place the cherries in the dish.

In a large mixing bowl, whisk together the eggs and sugar until well combined. Add the flour and salt and whisk again, then slowly pour in the milk, whisking as you go, until you have a smooth batter. Pour the batter over the cherries, transfer the dish to the oven and bake for 30 minutes or until lightly golden and the batter has set.

Allow the clafoutis to cool slightly, then dust with some icing sugar and serve.

Serves 6

500 g (1 lb 2 oz) cherries, pitted
3 eggs
50 g (1¾ oz) caster (superfine) sugar
30 g (1 oz) plain (all-purpose) flour
pinch of salt
500 ml (2 cups) full-cream (whole) milk
icing (confectioners') sugar, for dusting

GALATOPITA

Galatopita is an elegant milk pie from Northern Greece, with a delightful crispy pastry base and luscious custard that's perfect for lazy weekends spent with family and friends. I have added lemon and raspberries, which I adore, but blueberries are wonderful as well. If you're short on time, you can make the pie using store-bought filo pastry – simply use six sheets of pastry, brushed with melted butter between each sheet.

✻

To make the filo pastry, place the flour and salt in a large bowl and mix well. Make a well in the centre and pour in the olive oil and white wine vinegar. Mix together with your hands, adding the warm water as you go, until you have a soft dough (you may need a little more or less water, so add it gradually rather than all at once).

Tip the dough onto a floured work surface and knead lightly until smooth, then place back in the bowl, cover with a tea towel and allow to rest for 1 hour.

Preheat the oven to 180°C (350°F) fan-forced. Lightly grease a 24 cm (9½ in) round baking dish.

Cut the dough in half, then wrap one half in plastic wrap and store in the fridge or freezer (see Note).

Roll out the remaining half of dough on a work surface lightly dusted with cornflour to a 30 cm (12 in) circle, then transfer to the prepared dish – you should have at least 2 cm (¾ in) of overhanging pastry.

Heat the milk in a large saucepan over medium heat until just before it starts to boil.

In a bowl, combine the semolina, eggs, vanilla extract, sugar, lemon zest and salt and whisk well. Using a ladle, pour in some of the hot milk and whisk until smooth, then pour the mixture into the remaining hot milk in the pan and stir until thickened. Remove the pan from the heat, add the butter and stir until melted.

Spread the semolina custard over the filo pastry and smooth the top with a spatula. Fold the overhanging pastry onto the custard to create an edge. Scatter the raspberries on top, then transfer to the oven and bake for 30–35 minutes, until the pastry is golden.

Remove the pie from the oven and allow it to cool and set. Serve at room temperature.

Serves 6

1 litre (4 cups) full-cream (whole) milk
120 g (4½ oz) fine semolina
2 eggs
1 teaspoon natural vanilla extract
150 g (5½ oz) caster (superfine) sugar
zest of 1 lemon
pinch of salt
75 g (2¾ oz) butter
150 g (5½ oz) raspberries

Filo pastry

300 g (2 cups) plain (all-purpose) flour, plus extra for dusting
1 teaspoon salt
80 ml (⅓ cup) olive oil
1 tablespoon white wine vinegar
about 250 ml (1 cup) lukewarm water
cornflour (cornstarch), for dusting

Note *This recipe makes twice the amount of pastry that you'll need for this pie, so store the remaining half in the fridge, tightly wrapped in plastic wrap, for a day, or in the freezer for 2–3 months; thaw overnight in the fridge before using.*

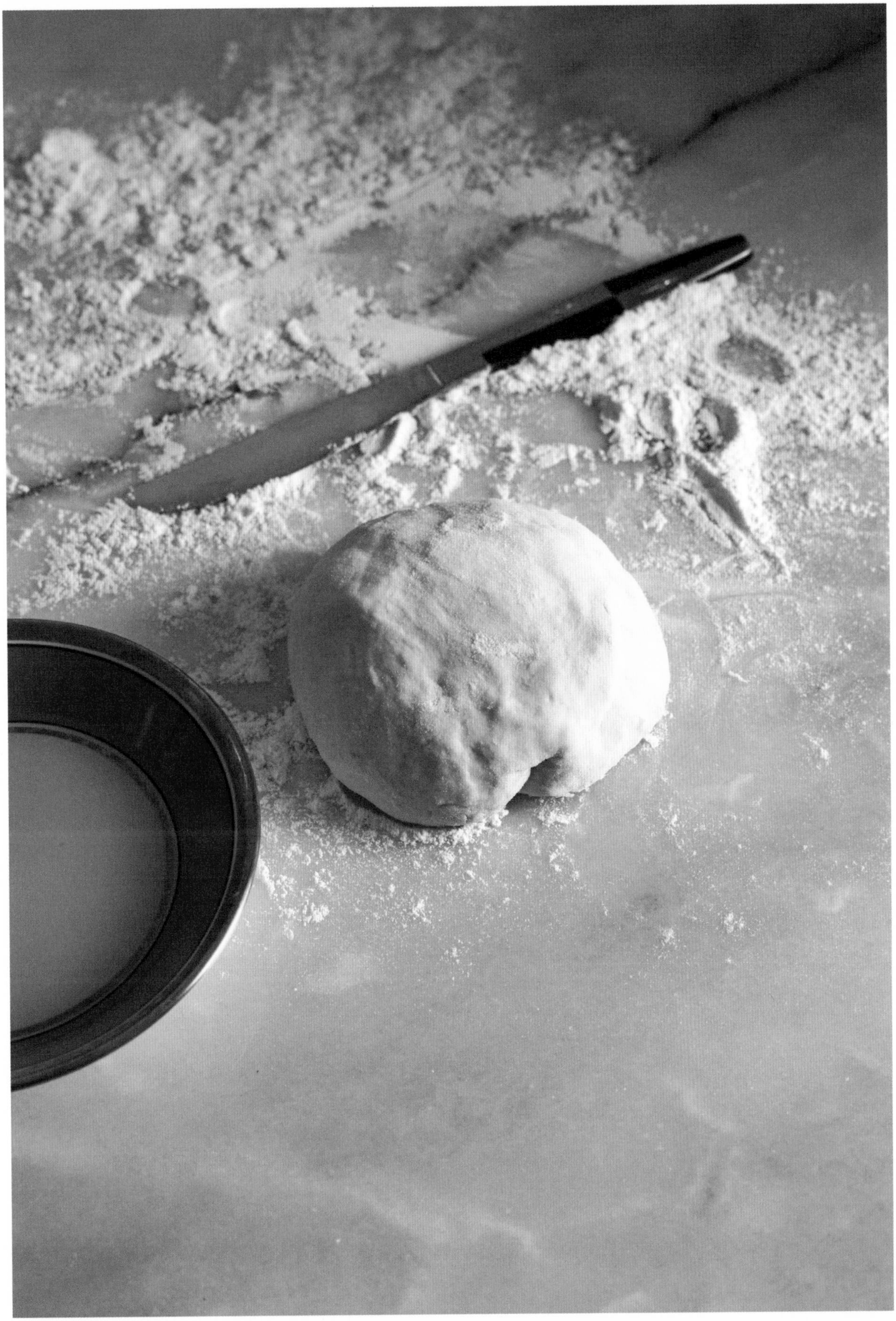

AUTUMN — WINTER

Autumn is my favourite season. The days are becoming shorter, the nights are cooler and the leaves are changing colour from their once lively greens to hues of red, orange and yellow, falling to the ground and rustling beneath your feet.

It was the beginning of autumn on a recent trip to Greece, and the warm days of the late Mediterranean summer still lingered. I stayed with my cousin, Antoni, and his wife, Eleni, in a small village on the outskirts of Florina in Thessaloniki. Their home was cosy and welcoming, with friends and relatives passing by on their daily walk, or popping in to say hello and staying for a while.

Even at this time of year, Antoni and Eleni's garden was mesmerising: daily eggs from the free-roaming chickens; and honey from the beehive to drizzle into cups of herbal tea or over a bowl of Greek yoghurt. In the outdoor kitchen, the aroma of charred red peppers (capsicums) and eggplants (aubergines) filled the air.

As the season came to an end, the preserving began: jars of pickles and bottled tomatoes started to line the shelves; garlic bulbs were plaited and strung up next to drying bunches of oregano; while pitchers of olives and barrels of olive oil ensured that there would be enough for the winter months, and just a little bit more.

At home, I look forward to gorgeous jammy figs, apples, pears and oranges; dark, leafy greens; earthy mushrooms and, perhaps for a treat, truffles. Market stalls display magnificent chestnuts, cauliflowers, leeks and cabbages, while beautiful citrus brings brightness to autumn days and myriad dishes.

As autumn fades away, the crispness of winter begins to settle in. It is a time of cosiness and warmth and a chance to slow down; a time for comforting soups, stews and braises, and pies, both savoury and sweet. I put on a sweater and think fondly of that autumn in Greece and the memories of food and love, surrounded by family.

127

CELERY AVGOLEMONO

This dish is typically made with pork and is one that my mother made quite often, but I like to make celery the hero ... it's mild, earthy and slightly peppery taste goes so well with the tangy avgolemono sauce. Use the tender leaves as well – most people tend to discard them, but they are lovely.

The delicate avgolemono is mostly known as the sauce for the classic Greek chicken soup of the same name, but it is also luscious as a dressing for dolmades and sarma (stuffed cabbage leaves), as well as a sauce served with roast chicken.

*

Trim the celery and set aside the small and tender leaves. Cut the stalks into 5 cm (2 in) pieces. Wash the leeks well to remove any sand or dirt, then pat dry and slice finely.

Heat the olive oil in a large saucepan over medium heat, add the onion and leek and saute for about 4 minutes, until softened. Add the celery and 1.5 litres (6 cups) of water, then cover with a lid and simmer for 20–30 minutes, until the celery is cooked through. Turn off the heat.

To make the avgolemono sauce, in a bowl, beat the egg whites using a hand whisk or fork until frothy, then add the yolks and continue to whisk, until you have a creamy consistency. Whisking constantly, add the lemon juice, a little at a time, until completely incorporated. Using a ladle, slowly add a ladleful of the celery broth to the beaten egg, whisking as you go, until combined. Add another two ladlefuls of broth, then pour the egg and lemon sauce into the celery broth and stir through slowly, either using a wooden spoon or by gently shaking the pan from side to side.

Spoon the creamy celery avgolemono onto a serving platter and scatter with the dill. Season well with salt and pepper and serve.

Serves 4

1 bunch of celery
2 leeks, white and pale green parts only,
    outer layers removed
90 ml (3 fl oz) olive oil
1 brown onion, diced
½ small bunch of dill, fronds picked
salt and pepper, to taste

Avgolemono sauce

2 eggs, separated
juice of 2 lemons

Note   *If you have excess celery, blanch the stalks in boiling water for a few minutes, then drain and freeze in an airtight container, ready to be added to dishes where it is cooked, such as this one.*

ROAST PUMPKIN & CHESTNUT SOUP

When I was young, my family would pack a picnic basket full of homemade filo pies, drinks and a thermos of coffee, and set off with friends to a peaceful spot where we knew we could collect chestnuts. Once we had finished lunch, the foraging would commence – searching under trees we would find chestnuts in clusters, peeking out from the fallen leaves, sometimes cracking their prickly shells open with our shoes.

Whenever I make this soup, I think of this childhood memory – it is so special to me and reminds me of the simple joys in life. The pairing of sweet roasted pumpkin and chestnuts is pure comfort in a bowl.

✳

Preheat the oven to 200°C (400°F) fan-forced.

Place the pumpkin and onion on a baking tray, drizzle with the olive oil and roast for 30 minutes or until soft and golden.

Transfer the pumpkin and onion to a large saucepan, along with the potato and about 750 ml (3 cups) of cold water. Bring to the boil over medium–high heat, then reduce the heat to a simmer and cook for 30 minutes, until the potato is tender. Stir through half the chestnuts and all of the milk, and season well with salt and pepper.

Using a blender, blitz the soup until silky smooth, then stir through most of the remaining chestnuts, reserving a small handful for garnish.

Divide the soup among bowls, drizzle with a little extra olive oil and swirl through a spoon of double cream, if desired. Scatter with the remaining chestnuts and a little shaved parmesan (if using). Crack over some black pepper, and serve.

Serves 4

500 g (1 lb 2 oz) pumpkin (winter squash), chopped into large chunks
1 red onion, quartered
80 ml (⅓ cup) olive oil, plus extra for drizzling
2 potatoes, peeled and cut into chunks
200 g (7 oz) frozen or tinned chestnuts, roughly chopped
200 ml (7 fl oz) full-cream (whole) milk
salt and pepper, to taste
double (heavy) cream, to serve (optional)
shaved parmesan, to serve (optional)

131

WHITE BEAN SOUP

White bean soup has been cooked in kitchens throughout the Mediterranean for hundreds of years. Greek fasolada, Italian zuppa di fagioli, French soupe au pistou and Spanish fabada asturiana being just some interpretations, with each cuisine using local ingredients to make this special dish their own.

I've kept my white bean soup vegetarian – it's not only nourishing, but simple to put together. To make it even easier and to save time, you can use tinned cannellini beans. Silverbeet (Swiss chard) or kale are also lovely added to this soup.

✻

If using dried beans, drain and rinse them well.

Heat the olive oil in a large saucepan over medium heat, add the onion and saute for 3–4 minutes, until softened. Add the garlic, carrot and celery and saute for 2 minutes or until the aroma of garlic fills your kitchen. Add the tomatoes and beans, stir well to combine, then cover with 1.5 litres (6 cups) of cold water. Add the bay leaves and bring to the boil, then reduce the heat to a simmer and cook for about 1 hour, adding more water if needed to maintain a soup consistency, until the beans are cooked through. (If you are using tinned beans, rinse and drain them, then add to the soup and cook for 15–20 minutes.) Season well with salt and pepper.

Divide the soup among bowls, top with a sprinkling of parsley (if using) and an extra drizzle of olive oil, and serve with fresh crusty bread, feta, olives and your choice of pickled vegetables.

Serves 4

500 g (1 lb 2 oz) dried cannellini beans (soaked in cold water overnight; you can also use 2 x 400 g/14 oz tins cannellini beans if you prefer)
60 ml (¼ cup) olive oil, plus extra for drizzling
1 brown onion, finely diced
2 garlic cloves, finely diced
2 small carrots, cut into chunks
2 celery stalks, sliced
1 × 400 g (14 oz) tin diced tomatoes
2 dried bay leaves
salt and pepper, to taste

To serve

chopped parsley leaves (optional)
crusty bread
crumbled Greek feta
kalamata olives
pickled vegetables

Goes with   *Serve this soup with Su boregi (see page 178), Potato, cheese & egg peinirli (see page 175) or Pispilita (see page 189) for a hearty supper.*

Note   *Cannellini beans freeze well. Simply soak a double quantity of beans, then drain and divide the beans you're not going to use into meal-sized portions and place into zip-lock bags. They will keep in the freezer for up to 3 months, ready to add to soups and stews.*

GREEN MINESTRONE

The classic Italian minestrone but with a twist. Traditionally, minestrone is simmered in a rich tomato broth, but here I maintain a white base and lean heavily on earthy winter greens and scented herbs, topped with shaved parmesan. Not only is this minestrone nutritious and full of flavour, it's perfect for using up any green vegetables that might be languishing in the crisper drawer. It's also easily adapted for the warmer seasons – simply swap out the winter veg for summer produce, or replace any of the vegetables here with your favourites.

❉

Heat the olive oil in a large saucepan over medium–high heat, add the onion and saute for 3–4 minutes, until softened. Add the garlic and cook for 2 minutes, then add the spring onion, celery, leek and potato and cook for a further 2 minutes.

Add the beans to the pan and cover with 2 litres (2 qts) of cold water. Bring the mixture to the boil and stir in the pasta, then cook until the pasta is al dente. Stir through the bay leaf, oregano, peas and greens and cook for 5–6 minutes, until the greens have wilted. Season well with salt and pepper.

Divide the soup among shallow bowls and top with the parsley, celery leaves and some shaved parmesan. Finish with an extra drizzle of olive oil and serve.

Serves 4

80 ml (⅓ cup) olive oil, plus extra
    for drizzling
1 brown onion, diced
2 garlic cloves, finely chopped
2 spring onions (scallions), finely sliced
2 celery stalks, diced, plus celery leaves
    to serve
1 leek, white and pale green parts only,
    washed well and sliced
1 potato, roughly chopped
1 × 400 g (14 oz) tin cannellini beans,
    rinsed and drained
150 g (5½ oz) ditalini or any tiny pasta
1 dried bay leaf
½ teaspoon dried oregano
155 g (1 cup) frozen peas
large handful of greens, such as kale
    or collard greens, roughly chopped
salt and pepper, to taste
small bunch of parsley, leaves picked
shaved parmesan, to serve

136

Goes with   *Savoury pastries and pies: the Su boregi on page 178, Potato, cheese & egg peinirli on page 175 or Pispilita on page 189 are ideal matches for this winter soup to make it a complete meal.*

LENTIL SOUP

Winter is a time for warming, soothing meals, and this humble lentil soup with familiar ingredients is one I turn to often. It may seem odd to add vinegar to a soup, but it pairs particularly well with lentils, adding a fresh vibrancy that would otherwise be missing. I encourage you to try it, as it takes this soup to another level.

❋

Rinse the lentils well under cold running water, then set aside to drain.

Heat the olive oil in a large saucepan over medium heat, add the onion and saute for 4–5 minutes, until softened. Add the garlic and saute for 2 minutes or until its aroma fills your kitchen, then add the carrot, celery, grated tomato, bay leaf, cumin, parsley, oregano and cinnamon stick, and stir well to combine. Add the lentils, season well with salt and pepper and cover with 1.5 litres (6 cups) of water. Bring the mixture to the boil, then reduce to a simmer and cook for 1 hour or until the lentils are soft and the soup has thickened. Remove from the heat and stir through the red wine vinegar.

Serve the soup hot, with an extra drizzle of olive oil, and crusty bread for dipping.

Serves 4

300 g (10½ oz) brown lentils

80 ml (⅓ cup) olive oil, plus extra for drizzling

1 large brown onion, diced

2 garlic cloves, finely chopped

1 carrot, diced

1 celery stalk, diced

4 tomatoes, grated

1 fresh bay leaf

½ teaspoon ground cumin

2 tablespoons finely chopped parsley

1 teaspoon dried oregano

1 cinnamon stick

salt and pepper, to taste

80 ml (⅓ cup) red wine vinegar

crusty bread, to serve

139

Make ahead *You can make this soup up to 3 days in advance and store in an airtight container in the fridge. It also freezes well for up to 2 months.*

Goes with *Serve this soup with Su Boregi (see page 178), Potato, cheese & egg penirili (see page 175) or Pispilita (see page 189).*

PASTA E FAGIOLI

Pasta & bean soup

Pasta e fagioli is a classic Italian pasta and bean soup that's often referred to as a peasant dish due to the soup's staple ingredients that can be found in most pantries. Not only is it warm and nourishing, it is also healthy and filling.

✦

If using dried beans, drain and rinse them well, then transfer to a large saucepan, cover with cold water and bring to the boil. Reduce the heat to a simmer and cook for 1½ hours or until the beans are soft, adding more water if necessary. Drain and set aside. Skip this step if using tinned beans.

Heat the olive oil in a large saucepan over medium heat, add the onion and saute for 2 minutes or until starting to soften. Add the garlic and cook for 2 minutes or until golden, then add the celery, carrot, tomato passata, bay leaves, oregano and 1 litre (4 cups) of water. Bring the mixture to the boil and add the pasta, then reduce the heat to a simmer and cook until the pasta is almost al dente. Add the beans and chilli flakes (if using), and continue to cook for 10 minutes. Season well with salt and pepper.

Divide the pasta e fagioli among bowls and serve with an extra drizzle of olive oil and shaved parmesan scattered over the top.

Serves 4–6

250 g (9 oz) dried cannellini beans, soaked in cold water overnight (or 1 × 400 g/14 oz tin cannellini beans, rinsed and drained)
60 ml (¼ cup) olive oil, plus extra for drizzling
1 brown onion, finely diced
2 garlic cloves, finely chopped
1 celery stalk, sliced
1 carrot, diced
250 g (1 cup) tomato passata (pureed tomatoes)
2 dried bay leaves
1 teaspoon dried oregano
250 g (9 oz) small pasta, such as ridged elbows
pinch of chilli flakes (optional)
salt and pepper, to taste
shaved parmesan, to serve

140

"At its heart, the Mediterranean
diet is more than just a collection
of foods, it is a way of life."

THE IMPORTANCE OF COMMUNITY

The Mediterranean diet has gained widespread recognition for its
numerous health benefits, but it is so much more than food. It is
a lifestyle steeped in a tradition of hospitality and community and,
for me, this is just as important as the celebrated cuisines that
surround the Mediterranean coastline.

This affirmation of community is the foundation of food and
culture throughout the region. It is a holistic approach – you can't
have food without friends and family coming together to enjoy
the meal that's been prepared. It is a time for sharing stories and
connecting, providing a sense of belonging and emotional well-being,
reducing feelings of isolation and loneliness. It's this emphasis on
sharing meals with family and friends, with generous tables of bread,
cheese, olives, a pickle or two, a few dishes to share and a wine
to match the flavours on offer, that really make the Mediterranean
diet one of the finest in the world.

I recall with great joy being at a festival in the village where
my father was born in Northern Greece. There were tables lined
with platters of regional delicacies, karafes of local wine, a band
playing in the village square and people, both young and old, dancing.
The soul-stirring music caught me off guard – enveloping me in its
embrace – and without warning, I felt a strong sense of belonging
within the community. It was a truly perfect experience and one
I will never forget.

At its heart, the Mediterranean diet is more than just
a collection of foods, it is a way of life that focuses on social
connections, shared meals and the celebration of produce
as a source of enjoyment and nourishment.

143

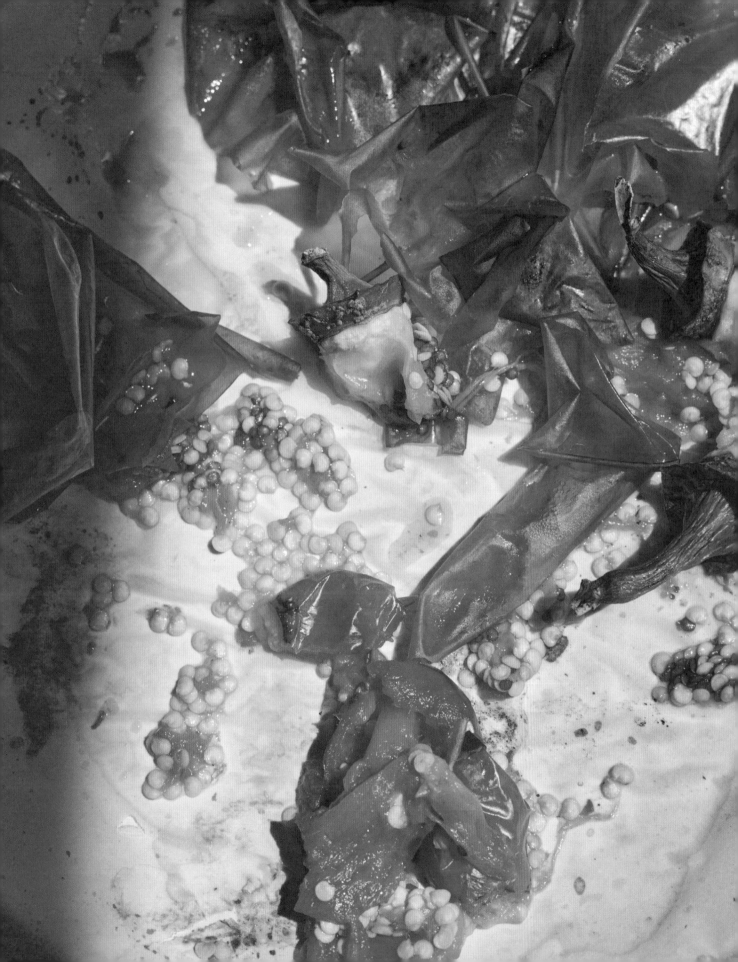

CAULIFLOWER FRITTERS WITH YOGHURT SAUCE

Cauliflower is a vegetable that I often serve as a salad, boiled and dressed with an olive oil and lemon dressing. In this recipe, I've put cauliflower to a different use to make these aromatic fritters, served with a refreshing yoghurt sauce. You will notice that the onion is used raw in the fritters, which adds a lovely crunch when you bite into them. This dish has become one of my favourite ways to celebrate this humble vegetable.

❋

Place the cauliflower in a large saucepan, cover with cold water and bring to the boil. Reduce the heat to a simmer and cook for 5–6 minutes, until tender. Drain the cauliflower, then transfer to a large bowl and use the back of a fork to break down the florets. Set aside to cool.

Prepare the yoghurt sauce by stirring the ingredients together in a bowl. Season to taste.

In a large bowl, combine the onion, garlic, eggs, flour, cumin, cinnamon and parsley. Gently whisk to mix well and season with salt and pepper. Add the cooled cauliflower and combine well.

Heat the olive oil in a large frying pan over high heat. For each fritter, spoon about 3 tablespoons of the cauliflower mixture into the oil. Continue in small batches, but don't overcrowd the pan as this will lower the heat of the oil.

Shallow-fry the fritters for about 3 minutes on each side, flattening them slightly with a spatula as they cook, until golden. Drain on paper towel.

Place the fritters on a serving plate, scatter over some parsley leaves and serve warm with the yoghurt sauce and lemon wedges.

Serves 4

1 small cauliflower (about 400 g/14 oz), cut into florets
1 small brown onion, finely diced
1 garlic clove, finely diced
3 eggs
100 g (⅔ cup) plain (all-purpose) flour
1 teaspoon ground cumin
1 teaspoon ground cinnamon
2 tablespoons finely chopped parsley, plus extra leaves to serve
salt and pepper, to taste
250 ml (1 cup) olive oil, for shallow-frying
lemon wedges, to serve

Yoghurt sauce

300 g (10½ oz) Greek-style yoghurt
1 garlic clove, minced
zest of ½ lemon, plus all the juice

146

LEEKS WITH ROMESCO

Romesco is a classic Catalan sauce made from red peppers, almonds, bread and olive oil, and typically served with smoky charred calçots, which are native to the region, as well as fish, chicken and meat. Calçots are sweet and delicate onions somewhere between a spring onion (scallion) and a leek, the latter of which makes a good substitute for these hard-to-find alliums. The sweetness of the sauce pairs perfectly with leeks, but it's also delicious with other roasted vegetables, especially eggplant (aubergine), cauliflower and potatoes, as well as eggs and, of course, simply spread on crusty bread!

If you love roasted red peppers, as I do, you will absolutely become addicted to this romesco sauce.

✻

Preheat the oven to 180°C (350°F) fan-forced.

Wash the leeks well to remove any sand or dirt, then pat dry.

Heat a chargrill pan over high heat and place the leeks directly in the pan (cut them in half crossways if they're very long). Cook the leeks, turning regularly, for 12–14 minutes, until charred and beginning to soften – the leeks will release some liquid as they cook. Remove from the heat and place the leeks on a serving platter – they will continue to soften as they rest and cool.

To make the romesco sauce, place the peppers on a baking tray and roast in the oven, turning occasionally, for 30–45 minutes, until blackened all over. Set aside until cool enough to handle, then peel and remove the seeds. Tear the flesh into strips and set aside. Skip this step if using jarred peppers.

Toast the almonds in a dry frying pan over medium–high heat for 3–4 minutes, until golden around the edges. Remove from the heat and set aside.

Heat the olive oil in the same frying pan over low heat, add the bread and fry for 2–3 minutes, until golden on both sides. Remove the bread from the pan and tear into pieces.

Add the onion to the pan and saute over medium heat for 3–4 minutes, until softened, then add the tomato and 125 ml (½ cup) of water and simmer for 12–15 minutes, until slightly thickened. Remove from the heat and allow to cool.

Using a mortar and pestle or a small blender, crush the garlic with a pinch of salt. Add the toasted almonds and pound or blend until finely crushed. Add the toasted bread, red peppers, paprikas, cooled tomato mixture and red wine vinegar and pound or blend until you have a slightly chunky sauce, adding a little water if the mixture is very thick. Season to taste with more red wine vinegar, salt and pepper, and serve the romesco sauce alongside the leeks.

Serves 4

4 leeks, white and pale greens
     parts only, outer layers removed

Romesco sauce

4 red peppers (capsicums), or use
     jarred whole roasted red peppers
100 g (⅔ cup) almonds
60 ml (¼ cup) olive oil
2 slices crusty white bread
½ brown onion, finely diced
3 tomatoes, finely chopped
2 garlic cloves
salt and pepper, to taste
1 teaspoon sweet paprika
1 teaspoon smoked paprika
splash of red wine vinegar,
     plus extra to taste

149

DOLMADES

Meze is so much more than food, it's a Mediterranean lifestyle, and dolmades are the perfect meze dish.

I like to use pre-blanched jarred vine leaves as it does save a little work; however, if you do have fresh leaves, simply rinse them well, then stack and roll them loosely and blanch in a saucepan of boiling water for a couple of minutes, until softened.

❖

Heat the olive oil in a frying pan over medium heat, add the onion and saute for 3–4 minutes, until softened. Add the rice and tomato and stir to coat the rice in the onion mixture. Pour in 500 ml (2 cups) of water and simmer for 10–12 minutes, until the rice is cooked through. Remove from the heat and add the pine nuts, currants, parsley, mint, cinnamon and cloves. Season well with salt and pepper and stir to combine the ingredients.

Line the base of a large saucepan with six of the vine leaves – this prevents the dolmades from burning.

Lay a vine leaf, vein side down, on your work surface and add 1 tablespoon of the rice mixture to the middle of the leaf. Fold the sides of the leaf over the filling, then, starting with end closest to you, roll up the leaf to enclose the filling. Gently squeeze the dolmade in the palm of your hand, then place in the pan. Continue until you have used all of the filling and vine leaves, then pour enough water into the pan to come halfway up the side of the dolmades and drizzle with a little extra olive oil and a sprinkle of salt. Place a small heatproof plate on top of the dolmades to keep them in place, then bring to a simmer over low heat and cook for 30 minutes.

Serve the dolmades cold with a dollop of yoghurt and lemon wedges as part of a meze. They are also lovely with the avgolemono sauce on page 128.

Makes 24

60 ml (¼ cup) olive oil, plus extra
    for drizzling
1 brown onion, diced
200 g (7 oz) short-grain rice
1 tomato, grated
2 tablespoons pine nuts
2 tablespoons currants
2 tablespoons finely chopped parsley leaves
1 tablespoon finely chopped mint leaves
½ teaspoon ground cinnamon
¼ teaspoon ground cloves
salt and pepper, to taste
30 fresh or jarred vine leaves
Greek-style yoghurt, to serve
lemon wedges, to serve

150

SPINACH FRICASSEE

Fricassee, born in France and now a star in many
Greek dishes served with the classic avgolemono sauce,
is traditionally made with chicken or veal, but also works
very well with just vegetables. The word 'fricassee' literally
means to cut up, fry and braise in a sauce, and in this
recipe I've applied the technique to spinach, zucchini
and tomatoes. If you'd like to make it the Greek way,
omit the tomatoes and lemon zest and juice, and finish
the dish with the avgolemono sauce on page 128.

✻

Heat the olive oil in a large saucepan over medium heat, add
the onion and saute for 3–4 minutes, until golden. Add the grated
tomato and 375 ml (1½ cups) of water and simmer for 4–5 minutes.

Add the zucchini to the tomato sauce and stir to combine.
Add half the dill and all of the spinach, then cover with a lid,
reduce the heat to low and simmer for 15 minutes or until the
zucchini is tender.

Season the fricassee with salt and pepper and scatter the
remaining dill over the top. Finish with the lemon zest and juice,
and serve with feta and crusty bread.

Serves 4

80 ml (⅓ cup) olive oil

1 brown onion, finely diced

3 tomatoes, grated

3 zucchini (courgettes), sliced into 2 cm
(¾ in) thick rounds

½ bunch of dill, fronds picked

500 g (1 lb 2 oz) English spinach,
washed well and roughly chopped

salt and pepper, to taste

zest and juice of 1 lemon

Greek feta, to serve

crusty bread, to serve

154

Goes with   *Serve with the Paprika roast potatoes on page 166 to dip into
the fricassee sauce.*

CABBAGE SALAD WITH MINT & DRIED FIGS

The sweet, mild taste of cabbage makes it an excellent vegetable to use in salads. Here, I combine it with crisp and spicy radishes, sweet green peas and dried figs, which add a wonderfully chewy texture to this simple, but flavourful, dish.

*

If using fresh peas, blanch them in a saucepan of boiling water for 1 minute or until they rise to the top; if using frozen peas, boil for 30 seconds. Drain the peas, then refresh under cold running water and drain again.

Place the peas, cabbage, radish, parsley, mint and fig in a salad bowl and toss lightly to combine.

Combine the honey–mustard dressing ingredients in a small bowl and whisk until emulsified.

Pour the dressing over the cabbage salad and mix gently. Top with a generous amount of shaved kefalotyri and serve.

Serves 4

100 g (⅔ cup) fresh or frozen green peas
200 g (7 oz) white cabbage, finely sliced
4 radishes, finely sliced
1 tablespoon parsley leaves
1 tablespoon mint leaves
4 dried figs, diced
shaved kefalotyri, to serve

Honey–mustard dressing

1 tablespoon dijon mustard
1 tablespoon honey
125 ml (½ cup) olive oil
60 ml white balsamic vinegar
salt and pepper, to taste

157

Goes with   *I like to serve this salad with the Pastitsio on page 204.*

Make ahead   *The cabbage can be shredded and stored, tightly covered in a bowl or in a zip-lock bag in the fridge, for up to 2 days.*

ROCKET, FENNEL & ORANGE SALAD

Fresh, light and citrusy, this salad is delicious as a light lunch, or as a side to chicken, fish or meat. It's important to dress the salad just before serving in order to retain the crispness and crunch of the fennel. The sweetness of the figs is a great little addition.

❉

Working with one orange at a time, hold the orange over a bowl and use a small sharp knife to cut between the membranes of each segment and gently remove. Place the segments in a salad bowl and squeeze the remaining juice from the leftover membranes into the bowl beneath you.

Add the fennel and rocket to the orange segments and gently toss to combine. Arrange the figs (if using) over the salad.

To make the dressing, whisk together the ingredients in a small bowl, until emulsified. Drizzle the dressing over the salad, scatter with the mint leaves and serve.

158

Serves 4

2 oranges, peeled (you can also
 use mandarins)
1 fennel bulb, very finely sliced
 (use a mandoline if you have one)
150 g (5½ oz) rocket (arugula)
6 figs, quartered (optional)
small handful of mint leaves, to serve

Honey, mustard & orange dressing

1 tablespoon olive oil
1 tablespoon honey
1 teaspoon dijon mustard
2 tablespoons orange juice
 (from the segmented oranges)
salt and pepper, to taste

Goes with *I like to serve this salad with the Mushroom risoni on page 186 for an exquisite lunch.*

BAKED FRITTATA WITH GREENS & RICOTTA

The humble frittata is a canvas for so many flavours and a wonderful way to use up leftover veg in your fridge and pantry. Some of my favourite combinations include broccoli and feta; cauliflower; red peppers (capsicums) and spinach; mushrooms and herbs; tomatoes, basil and mozzarella; asparagus; or even the simple, but classic, potato and egg. There are so many wonderful variations!

✻

Preheat the oven to 180°C (350°F) fan-forced.

Heat the olive oil in a large cast-iron frying pan over medium heat, add the spring onion and saute for 4–5 minutes, until softened. Add the greens and cook for 2 minutes or until they start to wilt. Remove the pan from the heat, add the herbs and stir well to combine, then spread the mixture in an even layer in the pan and dot the ricotta over the top.

In a bowl, whisk together the eggs and season well with salt and pepper. Pour the egg over the greens and ricotta, then transfer to the oven and bake for 20–25 minutes, until the top is golden and the egg is set.

Remove the pan from the oven and scatter the frittata with a few extra parsley and basil leaves and a generous amount of shaved parmesan. Cut into slices and serve.

Serves 4

80 ml (⅓ cup) olive oil
3 spring onions (scallions), finely sliced
500 g (1 lb 2 oz) spinach
    (or a combination of spinach,
    kale and silverbeet/Swiss chard),
    roughly chopped
small handful of parsley leaves, roughly
    chopped, plus extra leaves to serve
small handful of basil leaves, roughly
    chopped, plus extra leaves to serve
200 g (7 oz) ricotta
8 eggs
salt and pepper, to taste
shaved parmesan, to serve

160

ROASTED CABBAGE WITH YOGHURT DRESSING

Roasting cabbage releases the vegetable's natural hints of sweetness and nuttiness that you otherwise don't experience when eating this vegetable raw. You can also barbecue the cabbage or cook it in a chargrill pan on the stovetop, if you prefer. The yoghurt dressing adds a burst of refreshing creaminess that's the perfect foil against the slightly charred cabbage.

✻

Preheat the oven to 200°C (400°F) fan-forced.

Slice the cabbage into 6–8 wedges and place on a baking tray. Drizzle both sides of the cabbage with olive oil, then transfer to the oven and roast, turning once, for 30–40 minutes, until tender and slightly charred.

To make the yoghurt dressing, whisk together the ingredients in a small bowl.

Transfer the cabbage to a serving platter and drizzle over the yoghurt dressing. Scatter with mint leaves and serve warm.

Serves 4–6

½ white cabbage
olive oil, for drizzling
mint leaves, to serve

Yoghurt dressing

120 g (4½ oz) Greek-style yoghurt
1 teaspoon honey
2 tablespoons olive oil
zest and juice of 1 lemon
salt and pepper, to taste

163

CHARRED BRUSSELS SPROUTS WITH WALNUTS & HONEY

Brussels sprouts belong to the cabbage family, and they resemble a tiny cabbage too. Earthy and slightly bitter when eaten raw, their flavour reveals a sweetness once roasted, pan-fried or charred. Here I've opted for the latter and added honey, which balances and mellows the smoky flavour of the charred sprouts. The walnuts add some welcome crunch to this winter side dish.

❊

Heat the olive oil in a large frying pan over medium heat and add the brussels sprouts. Season well with salt and pepper and saute for about 15 minutes, until the sprouts have softened and are starting to char in places. Add the honey and red wine vinegar and stir well, then simmer for about 4 minutes – the sauce will begin to thicken and become glossy.

Remove the pan from the heat and tumble the sprouts into a serving dish. Scatter over the walnuts and sprinkle with the lemon zest and a generous handful of grated parmesan, if desired.

Serves 4

80 ml (⅓ cup) olive oil

500 g (1 lb 2 oz) brussels sprouts, trimmed and halved

salt and pepper, to taste

115 g (⅓ cup) honey

60 ml (¼ cup) red wine vinegar

75 g (2¾ oz) walnuts, toasted

1 tablespoon grated lemon zest (optional)

grated parmesan, to serve (optional)

164

Goes with   *Pair the brussels sprouts with the Paprika roast potatoes on page 166 for a lovely light meal.*

PAPRIKA ROAST POTATOES

This was one of my mother's favourite ways to cook potatoes and now it's one of mine. The tomatoey sauce and generous sprinkling of paprika is reminiscent of Spanish patatas bravas, but with roasted potatoes instead of fried, making this a healthier rendition of the classic. A tablespoon of sweet paprika may seem like a lot, but it somehow makes these potatoes even more moreish. Feel free to swap in smoked paprika if you prefer a smoky flavour, or use half sweet and half smoked.

*

Preheat the oven to 200°C (400°F) fan-forced.

Place the potato in a large saucepan and cover with plenty of cold water. Bring to the boil over medium–high heat, then reduce the heat to a simmer and cook the potato for 7 minutes. Drain.

Pour the oil into a large baking tray, add the potato and toss to coat. Stir through the grated tomato, garlic, oregano and sweet paprika, and season well with salt and pepper.

Roast the potato for about 30 minutes, until tender and golden, then take to the table and serve.

Serves 4–6

1 kg (2 lb 3 oz) roasting potatoes,
   peeled and quartered
125 ml (½ cup) olive oil
4 tomatoes, grated
4 garlic cloves, unpeeled
2 teaspoons dried oregano
1 tablespoon sweet paprika
salt and pepper, to taste

Goes with   *These moreish potatoes are a treasured favourite and although I can enjoy them on their own, they are also perfect with saucy dishes to soak up the juices or as a side to grilled meats. Other dishes that pair well with these potatoes include the Charred brussels sprouts with walnuts & honey on page 164, Chestnut & wild mushroom stifado on page 203 and the Spinach fricassee on page 154.*

HOW TO PREPARE OLIVES

*I first attempted to brine olives after a friend kindly gifted
me a box from their own harvest. I knew I had to call my
Uncle Anastasi – a knowledgeable and skilled gardener with
a magnificent garden – he talked me through the process and
I took notes. Occasionally I would call if I needed clarification,
but he checked in as well, as he often did. He understood the
importance of passing down these traditions, and I remember
well the stories he would share from his childhood, learning
from his parents how to grow and preserve vegetables to enjoy
year-round.*

*Preserving olives requires patience and some effort, but
the fulfilment of preparing your own makes it so worthwhile.
From sorting and scoring, to changing the water daily,
the process is deeply immersed in ritual. Brined olives are
not only delicious but also rich in nutrients, making them
a healthy addition to your table.*

To start, sort through the olives and remove any leaves, stems and
fruit that is damaged. Using a small sharp knife, score three small
slits, lengthways, into each olive – this helps to preserve them and
draws out the bitterness in the fruit.

Place the olives in a large plastic tub or bucket and cover
with cold tap water. Place a large plate on top of the olives, to keep
them submerged, and change the water daily for 3–4 days, after
which time you can start adding the salt – I add 225 g (1 cup)
of coarse salt to every 2.4 litres (2.5 qts) of water. Cover the olives
with the brine, with a plate on top, and leave overnight, then
repeat this process, changing the brine daily, for about 2 weeks,
until the olives have lost nearly all their bitterness.

When the olives are ready to be bottled, tip them into clean,
sterilised jars (see page 21). Make another batch of brine in a
saucepan and bring to the boil, then remove from the heat and
allow to cool completely. Carefully pour the brine over the olives,

"Preserving olives requires patience and some effort, but the fulfilment of preparing your own makes it so worthwhile."

add a little olive oil to seal and pop the lids on. Store the jars in a cool, dark place for about 6 months, after which time they will be ready to use. They should keep for about 12 months.

When you are ready to use your olives, pour out the salty brine, replace with clean water and refrigerate. There should be enough salt in the olives to seep out into the water and create a weak, salty brine. You can add garlic, oregano and lemon juice at this stage, if you like, or any other preferred flavourings.

To eat, remove however many olives you need and cover them with some olive oil, a little fresh lemon juice or vinegar, garlic, black pepper and oregano and let them soak overnight before serving … delicious.

SPINACH GNOCCHI

Simple, comforting and perfect for dinner!

This recipe asks for 80 g (2¾ oz) of plain flour to make the gnocchi, but this can vary depending on how much water your spinach and ricotta are holding. Add the flour slowly until you reach the right consistency – you want them to be soft, but also firm enough to roll out.

❋

Place the spinach in a large saucepan and cover with water. Bring to the boil over medium heat and cook for 2 minutes or until the spinach has wilted. Drain the spinach and refresh in cold water, then set aside in a colander to drain and cool.

When the spinach is cool enough to handle, squeeze out the excess liquid and chop finely. Transfer to a large bowl and add the ricotta, grated parmesan, egg and nutmeg, then season well with salt and pepper and stir gently to combine. Slowly add the flour, mixing with a fork as you go, until you have a cohesive dough.

Place the dough on a lightly floured work surface and divide into four pieces. Working with one piece at a time, roll the dough into a long rope, about 2 cm (¾ in) thick. Cut the rope into 2 cm (¾ in) pieces and set aside. Repeat with the remaining dough.

Half-fill a saucepan with water and bring to the boil over medium heat. Add the gnocchi in small batches and cook until they rise to the top. Cook for a further minute, then use a slotted spoon to transfer the gnocchi to a serving dish. Repeat with the remaining gnocchi.

Meanwhile, make a quick sauce by heating the olive oil in a frying pan over medium heat. Add the cherry tomatoes and cook for 4–5 minutes, until starting to collapse. Spoon the tomatoes over the gnocchi and scatter with crumbled feta or shaved parmesan and a few basil leaves. Finish with an extra drizzle of olive oil and some black pepper, and serve.

Serves 4

500 g (1 lb 2 oz) English spinach, washed well and roughly chopped
200 g (7 oz) ricotta
50 g (½ cup) grated parmesan
1 egg
¼ teaspoon freshly grated nutmeg
salt and pepper, to taste
80 g (2¾ oz) plain (all-purpose) flour, plus extra for dusting
80 ml (⅓ cup) olive oil, plus extra for drizzling
200 g (7 oz) cherry tomatoes
crumbled Greek feta or shaved parmesan, to serve
basil leaves, to serve

POTATO, CHEESE & EGG PEINIRLI

The peinirli is a boat-shaped open pie with a dough that's similar to a traditional pizza and calzone crust, the difference being that peinirli dough is thicker and fluffier. They are traditionally filled with lots of cheese, but I find that the combination of potato, cheese and egg elevates these rustic pies to rival any Italian pizza.

❋

To make the dough, in a large bowl, whisk together 75 g (½ cup) of the flour, the yeast, sugar and enough of the warm water to make a paste. Set aside for 15 minutes or until you see bubbles forming on the surface. Add the remaining flour and warm water, the salt, olive oil and warm milk and mix to form a shaggy dough. Transfer to a lightly floured work surface and knead for about 8 minutes, until the dough is smooth and no longer sticky.

Brush a large clean bowl with olive oil and add the dough. Cover with a tea towel and allow to sit for about 1 hour, until the dough has doubled in size.

Preheat the oven to 200°C (400°F) fan-forced. Line a large baking tray with baking paper.

Peel and very finely slice the potatoes, then place in a bowl of cold water to prevent them discolouring. Combine the cheese and parsley in a separate bowl and season to taste with salt and pepper.

Tip the dough onto a floured work surface and punch it down to knock the air out, then knead for a few minutes. Cut the dough into six equal pieces and shape them into balls.

Roll out each ball of dough into a 10 × 12 cm (4 × 4¾ in) rectangle, about 1–1.5 cm (½ in) thick.

Drain the potato, then layer the slices over the dough, leaving a 2 cm (¾ in) border. Scatter with the cheese mixture.

Shape the peinirli by rolling the long edges of the dough inwards to create a risen edge, then twist the short ends in opposite directions to form the classic 'boat' shape. Transfer to the prepared tray and bake for 15 minutes.

Remove the tray from the oven and use the back of a spoon to create an indent in the middle of the cheese mixture in each peinirli. Carefully crack an egg into each indent, then return the tray to the oven and cook for a further 5 minutes or until the egg whites have set and the peinirli are golden brown.

Brush the golden edges of the peinirli with a little melted butter and serve warm.

Note   *If you prefer, you can lightly beat three eggs into the grated cheese instead of adding an egg to the top of each peinirli.*

Serves 6

200 g (7 oz) potatoes
300 g (10½ oz) grated cheese, such as
    kasseri, gruyere, Greek feta, ricotta
    or mozzarella, or a combination
1 tablespoon finely chopped parsley
salt and pepper, to taste
6 eggs
melted butter, for brushing

Peinirli dough

500 g (3⅓ cups) plain (all-purpose)
    flour, plus extra for dusting
7 g (2 teaspoons) dried yeast
1 teaspoon sugar
200 ml (7 fl oz) warm water
1 teaspoon salt
1 tablespoon olive oil, plus extra
    for brushing
50 ml (1¾ fl oz) warm milk

175

PEA & RICOTTA-STUFFED CONCHIGLIE

It is said that stuffed pasta first appeared in Italian cuisine in the 1500s, where its popularity spread and infiltrated many cuisines throughout Europe, each with their own twist. The Greeks, who were influenced by Turkey's own filled pasta known as manti, which are traditionally filled with ground meat, onion and spices, mostly make and fill pasta with cheese, with half circles being the simplest shape to make. They are then either cooked in simmering water or baked until golden.

This is my favourite, go-to, easy dinner. For simplicity, I have used store-bought pasta shells; the sweetness of the peas, together with the ricotta, tomato and freshness of the lemon, is perfect.

❊

Preheat the oven to 180°C (350°F) fan-forced.

Add the pasta shells to a large saucepan of boiling water and cook according to the packet instructions, until al dente. Drain and set aside to cool.

While the pasta is cooking, prepare the filling. Heat the olive oil in a frying pan over medium heat, add the onion and sauté for 3–4 minutes, until softened. Add the garlic and saute for 2 minutes, then turn off the heat and add the peas, ricotta, yoghurt, nutmeg and lemon zest. Season well with salt and pepper and stir to combine the ingredients.

Spread 150 g (5½ oz) of the tomato passata in the base of a 25 cm (10 in) round baking dish. Using a tablespoon, fill each pasta shell with the pea and ricotta mixture and place in the baking dish in a single layer. Pour over the remaining tomato passata and sprinkle with the parmesan. Bake for 20–30 minutes, until golden.

Serves 4

250 g (9 oz) conchiglie (giant pasta shells)
3 tablespoons olive oil
1 small brown onion, finely diced
1 garlic clove, minced
200 g (7 oz) fresh or frozen peas
200 g (7 oz) ricotta
50 g (1¾ oz) Greek-style yoghurt
¼ teaspoon freshly grated nutmeg
zest of ½ lemon
salt and pepper, to taste
400 g (14 oz) tomato passata
   (pureed tomatoes)
50 g (½ cup) grated parmesan

SU BOREGI

Su boregi, or water borek, is one of Turkey's much-loved pastries that once you've tasted you will understand why it is so popular among Turkish communities … it is just so moreish, with crispy pastry on the outside and a soft vegetable and cheese-filled centre.

The original su boregi is made with feta and parsley and is a popular breakfast dish throughout Turkey, but I think it's wonderful any time of the day.

❁

Wash the leeks well to remove any sand or dirt, then pat dry and slice finely.

Heat 60 ml (¼ cup) of the olive oil in a frying pan over medium heat and add the leek and 125 ml (½ cup) of water. Simmer, stirring frequently, for 5–6 minutes, until the leek has softened and collapsed. Transfer the leek to a bowl, add the feta and season well with pepper. Stir to combine and set aside.

To make the water pastry, whisk the eggs in a large bowl with 1 tablespoon of water and the salt. Add the flour and mix well to form a shaggy dough. Tip the mixture onto a floured work surface and knead for about 8 minutes, until you have a smooth dough. Divide the dough into ten equal-sized balls and allow to rest, covered with a tea towel, for 20 minutes.

On a lightly floured work surface, roll each ball of dough into a 30 cm (12 in) circle, stacking them as you go and dusting with flour between each layer to prevent them sticking.

Preheat the oven to 200°C (400°F) fan-forced. Brush the base and side of a 5–6 cm (2–2½ in) deep, 26 cm (10¼ in) round baking tin with the remaining oil. Melt the butter in a small saucepan.

Bring a large saucepan of water to the boil, then reduce the heat to low. Place another pan of cold water next to the pan of boiling water. Working with one sheet of pastry at a time, carefully lower the pastry into the hot water and cook for 1 minute, then transfer to the pan of cold water to halt the cooking process. Place on a clean tea towel to dry and repeat with the remaining pastry.

Lay one pastry sheet in the prepared tin and brush with some of the melted butter. Repeat with another four sheets of pastry, then add the leek and feta mixture and spread it evenly over the pastry. Continue with the remaining pastry, brushing with butter in between each layer. Tuck any excess pastry into the side of the tin and pour over the remaining melted butter. Bake for 30–40 minutes, until golden brown.

Cut into wedges and serve warm.

Serves 4–6

4 leeks, white and pale green parts only,
    outer layers removed
100 ml (3½ fl oz) olive oil
250 g (9 oz) Greek feta, crumbled
black pepper, to taste
250 g (9 oz) butter

Water pastry

4 eggs
1 teaspoon salt
400 g (2⅔ cups) plain (all-purpose)
    flour, plus extra for dusting

PAPOUTSAKIA

Tomato & lentil-stuffed eggplant with cheese bechamel

This rich and comforting eggplant dish is my interpretation of the classic papoutsakia, which translates to 'little shoes' in Greek. It's traditionally prepared with minced (ground) beef, but I prefer to use brown lentils, as they soak up the tomato sauce beautifully and provide a textural balance to the rich and creamy cheese bechamel.

❋

Preheat the oven to 200°C (400°F) fan-forced.

Using a sharp knife, score the eggplant flesh deeply in a crisscross pattern, taking care not to pierce the skin. Drizzle with half the olive oil, season with some salt and pepper and place on a baking tray, cut side down. Roast in the oven for about 40 minutes, until softened. Set aside.

Meanwhile, heat the remaining olive oil in a frying pan over medium heat, add the onion and saute for 3–4 minutes, until softened. Add the garlic and cook for 1 minute, then add the tomatoes, lentils, cinnamon, cloves and cumin and saute for 4 minutes or until slightly reduced.

Gently scoop out half the eggplant flesh, leaving a 2 cm (¾ in) border around the edges, chop it roughly and add to the lentil mixture, stirring well to combine. Add the parsley and mint and stir through, then remove the pan from the heat.

Return the eggplant halves to the baking tray, cut side up, and, using a large spoon, fill the hollows with the lentil mixture.

To make the cheese bechamel, melt the butter in a large saucepan over medium heat. Add the flour and stir using a wooden spoon for a couple of minutes until the mixture is slightly golden. Add the milk, a little at a time and stirring constantly to avoid lumps forming, until completely incorporated. Add a generous amount of grated nutmeg and season well with salt and pepper. Continue to cook the bechamel, stirring occasionally, for about 10 minutes, until thickened and smooth. Remove the pan from the heat, add the egg and cheese, and stir well to combine and melt the cheese. Spoon the bechamel over the filled eggplant and bake for 30 minutes or until golden.

Serve with a simple green salad.

Serves 4

4 medium eggplants (aubergines),
  cut in half lengthways
100 ml (3½ fl oz) olive oil
salt and pepper, to taste
1 brown onion, finely diced
2 garlic cloves, minced
1 × 400 g (14 oz) tin diced tomatoes
250 g (9 oz) tinned brown lentils,
  rinsed and drained
½ teaspoon ground cinnamon
¼ teaspoon ground cloves
¼ teaspoon ground cumin
2 tablespoons chopped parsley leaves
1 tablespoon chopped mint leaves

Cheese bechamel

50 g (1¾ oz) butter
40 g (1½ oz) plain (all-purpose) flour
500 ml (2 cups) full-cream (whole) milk
large pinch of freshly grated nutmeg
salt and pepper, to taste
1 egg
120 g (4½ oz) kefalotyri or kasseri
  cheese, grated (you can also
  use gruyere)

181

ROOT VEGETABLE TAGINE WITH PRUNES

A tagine is so named for the conical-shaped earthenware pot that the dish is cooked in, which is designed to retain moisture and flavour. Traditional tagines are heat-treated for cooking, while others are purely decorative serving dishes. If using the former, make sure that your tagine is at room temperature before adding to a heat source, as placing a cold tagine on a hot surface may cause it to crack. Because tagines are designed to create steam as they cook, you don't need to add much liquid, but don't worry if you don't have one, a large saucepan or casserole dish (Dutch oven) make a perfectly acceptable replacement.

In this winter tagine, the vegetables are cooked with harissa, cumin, coriander, cinnamon and sweet prunes, traditional Moroccan ingredients that complement the earthy root veg. Serve with crusty bread or, as they do in Morocco, with some sweet, nutty couscous.

❁

Heat the olive oil in a tagine or large saucepan over medium heat, add the onion and garlic and saute for 3–4 minutes, until soft. Stir through the cumin, coriander and cinnamon and cook until their aroma fills your kitchen, then add the tomato, potato, carrot and sweet potato and stir well to coat the vegetables in the spices.

Add the chickpeas, harissa, prunes and 500 ml (2 cups) of water to the tagine or pan, then season well and bring to the boil. Reduce the heat to a simmer and cook for 20–25 minutes, until the vegetables are cooked through.

Serve in the tagine or transfer to a serving bowl if you've used a saucepan. Sprinkle over a little parsley and serve with lemon wedges and steamed couscous or crusty bread.

Serves 4

60 ml (¼ cup) olive oil
1 red onion, cut into wedges
2 garlic cloves, minced
1 teaspoon ground cumin
1 teaspoon ground coriander
1 teaspoon ground cinnamon
6 tomatoes, roughly chopped
3 potatoes, cut into chunks
2 carrots, thickly sliced
1 sweet potato, cut into chunks
1 × 400 g (14 oz) tin chickpeas
    (garbanzo beans), drained
1 tablespoon rose harissa
110 g (½ cup) pitted prunes,
    cut into quarters
salt and pepper, to taste
chopped parsley leaves, to serve
lemon wedges, to serve
steamed couscous or crusty bread,
    to serve

MUSHROOM RISONI

As summer gently fades, nature brings us its autumnal treasures and mushrooms begin to emerge with a range of flavours, shapes and textures. There are so many ways to celebrate mushrooms, and this risoni is the perfect comforting autumnal meal – heartwarming, meaty and full of flavour from the shiitake mushrooms.

❈

Heat the olive oil in a saucepan over medium heat, add the onion and saute for 3–4 minutes, until softened. Add the garlic and mushroom and saute for 5–6 minutes, until soft.

Add the risoni to the pan and stir well to coat the pasta in the mushroom mixture. Pour in the wine and stir for another 2 minutes. Add the stock or water slowly, stirring as you go, then reduce the heat to low and simmer for 12–15 minutes, until the risoni is cooked through.

Remove the pan from the heat and stir through the parsley and parmesan. Season to taste with salt and pepper, then divide the risoni among plates, top with shaved parmesan and extra pepper, and serve with lemon wedges on the side.

Serves 4

3 tablespoons olive oil
1 brown onion, finely diced
1 garlic clove, finely chopped
200 g (7 oz) shiitake or portobello
   mushrooms, sliced or chopped
   into chunks
250 g (9 oz) risoni
125 ml (½ cup) white wine
500 ml (2 cups) vegetable stock
   or water
1 tablespoon finely chopped
   parsley leaves
60 g (2 oz) parmesan, grated (you can
   also use pecorino, goat's cheese,
   gruyere or Greek feta), plus extra
   shaved parmesan to serve
salt and pepper, to taste
lemon wedges, to serve

Goes with   *I like to serve this dish with the Rocket, fennel & orange salad on page 158. It's light, fresh flavour is the perfect match for the richness of the mushroom risoni.*

PISPILITA

This gorgeous rustic pie originates from the mountainous region of Epirus in northwest Greece. The flavourful greens and herb filling is sandwiched between two layers of cornmeal crust that add a wonderful contrast to the pie's soft interior.

✻

Preheat the oven to 180°C (350°F) fan-forced.

To make the greens and herb filling, heat the olive oil in a large frying pan over medium heat, add the spring onion and saute for 2 minutes or until starting to soften. Add the greens and saute for 4 minutes or until the greens have wilted. Remove the pan from the heat, then stir through the feta, ricotta, eggs, herbs, lemon zest and nutmeg, and season well with salt and pepper. Mix gently to combine, then set aside.

Warm the milk and 500 ml (2 cups) of water in a large saucepan over medium heat. Rain in the cornmeal, stirring as you go, and cook, stirring, for 3–4 minutes, until the mixture is smooth and thickened. Season with salt and remove from the heat.

Pour half the cornmeal batter into a 40 cm (16 in) round baking tin (or similar) and spread the filling evenly over the top. Finish with the remaining cornmeal batter, smoothing the surface with the back of a spoon, then pour the beaten egg over the top of the pie. Transfer to the oven and bake for 50–60 minutes, until the pie is golden and set.

Cut the pie into squares and serve warm or at room temperature with a dollop of yoghurt on the side.

Serves 4

500 ml (2 cups) full-cream (whole) milk
300 g (2 cups) cornmeal
salt
2 eggs, lightly beaten
Greek-style yoghurt, to serve

Greens & herb filling

60 ml (¼ cup) olive oil
2 spring onions (scallions), finely chopped
500 g (1 lb 2 oz) greens, such as
    silverbeet (Swiss chard), kale, spinach
    or cavolo nero, roughly chopped
125 g (4½ oz) Greek feta, crumbled
100 g (3½ oz) ricotta
2 eggs
1 tablespoon finely chopped
    parsley leaves
1 tablespoon finely chopped mint leaves
1 teaspoon finely chopped dill fronds
zest of 1 lemon
½ teaspoon freshly grated nutmeg
salt and pepper, to taste

189

Goes with   *This cornmeal greens pie is so versatile when it comes to pairing it with other dishes, but I'm particularly fond of serving it with the Lentil soup on page 139 and the White bean soup on page 134.*

MUSHROOMS WITH KATSAMAKI

This earthy and hearty mushroom dish is delicious served with katsamaki, which is just like Italian polenta … in other words: heavenly comfort food.

Mushrooms have a great reputation for being a super food and a wonderful replacement for red meat. Use your favourite mushroom variety or a combination.

❊

Heat the olive oil in a frying pan over medium heat, add the onion and saute for 3–4 minutes, until softened. Add the garlic and cook for 2 minutes, then pour in the red wine. Add the mushroom and saute for 3–4 minutes, then add the thyme and butter and season well with salt and pepper.

Meanwhile, prepare the katsamaki. Pour 1 litre (4 cups) of water and the oil into a saucepan and bring to the boil. Slowly rain in the cornmeal, whisking constantly. Switch to a wooden spoon and continue to cook, stirring, for 5–6 minutes, until the mixture is thick and creamy and starts to come away from the side of the pan. Add the butter and stir through until melted, then remove from the heat and season well.

Spread the katsamaki onto a serving plate and top with the braised mushroom. Generously scatter shaved kefalotyri or pecorino and a few extra thyme leaves over the top, season with pepper, and serve.

Serves 4

60 ml (¼ cup) olive oil
1 brown onion, finely diced
2 garlic cloves, minced
125 ml (½ cup) red wine
750 g (1 lb 11 oz) mushrooms
    of your choice, roughly chopped
1 tablespoon thyme leaves,
    plus extra to serve
2 tablespoons butter
salt and pepper, to taste
shaved kefalotyri or pecorino,
    to serve

Katsamaki

60 ml (¼ cup) olive oil
120 g (4½ oz) fine cornmeal
40 g (1½ oz) butter
salt and pepper, to taste

ROASTED STUFFED MUSHROOMS

These roasted mushrooms, stuffed with salty and creamy feta, celery and red pepper, make the perfect light lunch, snack or main meal. I have used large portobello mushrooms here as they hold more of the filling, plus they are terrifically plump and meaty. Serve with a simple green salad.

✻

Preheat the oven to 200°C (400°F) fan-forced. Line a baking tray with baking paper.

Place the mushrooms, stalk-side down, on the prepared tray. Drizzle with a little olive oil, season well with salt and pepper and roast for 12–15 minutes, until they begin to soften.

While the mushrooms are roasting, saute the shallot in the olive oil in a frying pan over medium heat for 3–4 minutes, until softened. Add the garlic, celery and red pepper and saute for 5 minutes or until the vegetables have softened. Transfer the mixture to a large bowl and set aside to cool.

Add the feta, parsley and thyme to the cooled vegetable mixture and stir well.

Turn the mushrooms cup side up and evenly spoon the vegetable and feta mixture over the mushrooms. Top with the grated parmesan, then return the mushrooms to the oven and roast for a further 10 minutes or until the cheese is melted and golden.

Transfer the mushrooms to a serving platter, drizzle with a little extra olive oil and serve hot, with a green salad on the side.

Serves 4

8 large portobello mushrooms,
    stalks removed
60 ml (¼ cup) olive oil, plus extra
    for drizzling
salt and pepper, to taste
1 shallot, finely diced
1 garlic clove, finely chopped
1 celery stalk, diced
1 red pepper (capsicum), diced
200 g (7 oz) Greek feta, crumbled
    (or use a combination of your
    favourite cheeses)
1 teaspoon finely chopped parsley leaves
1 teaspoon finely chopped thyme leaves
50 g (½ cup) grated parmesan

192

LAHANORIZO

A celebration of the humble cabbage, this dish is a joy
to eat. I like to be generous with the sweet paprika –
it adds a slightly fruity and sweet flavour, with a hint
of pepperiness, that pairs beautifully with the earthy
cabbage and the freshness of the lemon. For a lighter
meal, add more cabbage and use less or no rice. It makes
a fantastic lunch or side to heartier dishes.

❋

Heat the olive oil in a large saucepan over medium–high heat, add
the onion and saute for 3–4 minutes, until soft. Add the shredded
cabbage and stir well to combine. Stir together the tomato paste
and 125 ml (½ cup) of water and add this to the pan, followed
by another 250 ml (1 cup) of water. Bring to the boil, then reduce
the heat to a simmer and cook for 20 minutes.

Add the rice to the pan, along with some more water if the
mixture is starting to look dry. Stir through the paprika and season
well with salt and pepper, then simmer for another 20–25 minutes,
until the rice and cabbage are cooked through and the water
is absorbed.

Divide the lahanorizo among plates, top with a sprinkling
of parsley and serve with lemon wedges on the side.

Serves 4

60 ml (¼ cup) olive oil
1 brown onion, finely diced
500 g (1 lb 2 oz) white cabbage,
    shredded
1 tablespoon tomato paste
    (concentrated puree)
120 g (4½ oz) medium-grain rice
1 teaspoon sweet paprika
salt and pepper, to taste
chopped parsley leaves, to serve
lemon wedges, to serve

195

ROASTED EGGPLANT WITH CANNELLINI BEANS

Eggplant is one of my most loved vegetables and it is the perfect vehicle for flavour and spices. It pairs so well with onions, garlic and tomato in this dish, as well as the legumes, with their delicate, creamy texture.

✳

If using dried beans, drain and rinse them, then place in a large saucepan and add enough cold water to cover them completely. Bring to the boil, then reduce the heat to a simmer and cook the beans, skimming any foam that rises to the top and adding more water if needed, for about 1 hour, until tender. Drain and set aside until needed. Skip this step if using tinned beans.

Meanwhile, preheat the oven to 200°C (400°F) fan-forced.

Place the eggplant on a baking tray, drizzle with half the olive oil and season well with salt. Roast for about 30 minutes, until softened. Set aside. Reduce the oven temperature to 180°C (350°F).

Pour the remaining olive oil into a flameproof casserole dish (Dutch oven) or roasting tin and set over medium heat. Add the onion and saute for 3–4 minutes, until softened. Add the garlic and cook for 1–2 minutes, until fragrant, then add the tomato, cumin, cinnamon and paprika, and stir well to combine. Stir through the cannellini beans and season well with salt and pepper, then nestle the eggplant among the bean mixture. Cover with a lid or foil, transfer to the oven and bake for 20 minutes, then remove the lid or foil and cook for a further 20 minutes, until the beans and eggplant are golden around the edges.

Remove the dish from the oven and sprinkle with chopped parsley and a generous squeeze of lemon.

Serve warm or at room temperature.

Serves 4

150 g (5½ oz) dried cannellini beans, soaked overnight (or use 1 × 400 g/ 14 oz tin cannellini beans, rinsed and drained)
4 medium eggplants (aubergines), sliced into quarters lengthways
125 ml (½ cup) olive oil
salt and pepper, to taste
1 brown onion, finely diced
2 garlic cloves, minced
6 tomatoes, chopped into chunks
1 tablespoon ground cumin
1 teaspoon ground cinnamon
1 teaspoon sweet paprika
chopped parsley leaves, to serve
freshly squeezed lemon juice, to serve

196

SARMA

Comforting and full of flavour, sarma is one of my favourite meals. There are many variations of this classic and elegant dish. It is usually made with minced (ground) meat and some like to use pickled cabbage instead of fresh. It can also be finished with a creamy avgolemono sauce (see page 128), but I prefer to serve these scrumptious cabbage rolls simply with a squeeze of lemon.

❄

Half-fill a large saucepan with water and bring to the boil. Cut the stem off the cabbage and use a small sharp knife to cut a cross in the base. Carefully lower the cabbage into the boiling water, then reduce the heat to a simmer and cook for about 12 minutes, until the leaves have softened. Lift out the cabbage, refresh under cold running water and drain in a colander. Separate the cabbage leaves and allow to cool. (If using pickled cabbage, place the leaves in a large bowl of water for about 5 minutes, then rinse and drain.)

Heat half the olive oil in a large frying pan over medium heat. Add the onion, carrot and garlic and saute for 4–5 minutes, until softened. Add the rice, 400 ml (13½ fl oz) of water, 2 tablespoons of the tomato paste, the paprika and sugar, and stir well to loosen the tomato paste. Simmer for 10 minutes, then remove the pan from the heat, stir through the parsley and season well.

Line the base of a large saucepan with two or three cabbage leaves. Using a small sharp knife, carefully shave the hard central stem from each cabbage leaf to make the leaves more pliable. Hold a leaf in the palm of one hand and add 2 tablespoons of the rice mixture to the middle of the leaf. Fold the leaf into a parcel, tucking in the sides to enclose the filling. Place the cabbage roll, seam side down, in the pan, then repeat with the remaining cabbage leaves and filling. Cover the cabbage rolls with 2–3 leaves of the remaining cabbage.

Combine the remaining tomato paste with 125 ml (½ cup) of water and pour this over the cabbage rolls, along with the remaining olive oil. Place a small heatproof plate on top of the rolls to keep them in place, then cover the pan with a lid and simmer over low heat, adding a little more water if the pan starts to look dry, for 1 hour or until cooked through. Serve the cabbage rolls with lemon wedges and an extra sprinkling of parsley.

198

Serves 4–6

1 white cabbage (or about 16 leaves
  of pickled cabbage)
125 ml (½ cup) olive oil
1 brown onion, finely diced
2 carrots, finely diced
2 garlic cloves, finely diced
400 g (14 oz) medium-grain rice
3 tablespoons tomato paste
  (concentrated puree)
1 tablespoon sweet paprika
1 teaspoon sugar
½ bunch of parsley, leaves picked
  and chopped, plus extra to serve
salt and pepper, to taste
lemon wedges, to serve

Leftover cabbage   *Keep the leftover leaves that are too small to fill and roll and use them to make a light salad – simply shred the leaves and drizzle with olive oil, sprinkle over a good amount of salt and a generous squeeze of lemon juice. You'll be surprised at how good it is.*

CHESTNUT & WILD MUSHROOM STIFADO

Stifado is a Greek stew made with small whole onions and aromatics, such as cinnamon, bay leaves and cloves, in a rich tomato and red wine sauce. The hint of sweetness and nutty flavour of the chestnuts, together with the earthy flavour of the mushrooms, creates a rich and comforting dish that's perfect served with potatoes, pasta, rice or crusty bread.

❖

Heat the olive oil in a saucepan over medium heat, add the onions and saute for 3–4 minutes, until golden and slightly caramelised.

Add the mushroom to the pan and cook for 10 minutes or until golden, then add the garlic and saute for 2 minutes. Add the tomatoes, chestnuts, bay leaves, cinnamon stick, cloves, red wine and red wine vinegar and bring to the boil, then reduce the heat to low and season well with salt and pepper. Cover with a lid and simmer for 30 minutes or until the onions are soft and the sauce has thickened.

Serve the stifado with your choice of potatoes, pasta, rice or crusty bread.

Serves 4

125 ml (½ cup) olive oil

12 baby onions, peeled and left whole

750 g (1 lb 11 oz) wild mushrooms, wiped clean and cut in half

2 garlic cloves, finely chopped

1 × 400 g (14 oz) tin diced tomatoes

250 g (9 oz) frozen or tinned chestnuts

2 dried bay leaves

1 cinnamon stick

8 cloves

125 ml (½ cup) red wine

60 ml (¼ cup) red wine vinegar

salt and pepper, to taste

203

Goes with   *Serve this stifado with the Paprika roast potatoes on page 166 to soak up the deliciously fragrant and aromatic sauce.*

PASTITSIO

Pastitsio is one of the great comfort foods of Greece, with each region having their own slight variation. Traditionally made with minced (ground) beef, this classic does take some time to put together, but it is worth every minute. Luscious and creamy eggplant, together with earthy lentils, sweet carrots, celery and a hint of cinnamon, I promise this will become a new favourite in your home.

✳

Preheat the oven to 200°C (400°F) fan-forced.

Cook the pasta in a large saucepan of boiling water until al dente. Drain and set aside.

Meanwhile, heat the olive oil in a large saucepan over medium heat. Add the onion and garlic and saute for 3–4 minutes, until softened. Add the celery and carrot and cook for 2 minutes, then add the eggplant, lentils, passata, bay leaves, oregano and ground cinnamon. Bring to a simmer and cook for 4–5 minutes, until well combined. Season to taste with salt and pepper.

To make the bechamel, melt the butter in a large saucepan over medium heat. Add the flour and stir using a wooden spoon for a couple of minutes until the mixture is slightly golden. Add the milk, a little at a time and stirring constantly to avoid lumps forming, until completely incorporated. Add the grated nutmeg and season well with salt and pepper. Continue to cook the bechamel, stirring occasionally, for about 10 minutes, until thickened and smooth. Remove the pan from the heat and add the egg and cheese, mixing well to combine.

To assemble the pastitsio, add half the pasta to a 25 × 35 cm (10 × 13¾ in) baking dish. Top with the tomato and lentil sauce, followed by the remaining pasta. Pour over the bechamel and spread evenly. Sprinkle with a little extra grated cheese and bake for about 45 minutes, until golden brown.

Serve with a green salad.

Serves 6

500 g (1 lb 2 oz) rigatoni or penne
60 ml (¼ cup) olive oil
1 brown onion, finely diced
2 garlic cloves, minced
1 celery stalk, finely diced
1 carrot, finely diced
1 eggplant (aubergine), cut into chunks
200 g (7 oz) tinned brown lentils, rinsed and drained
400 g (14 oz) tomato passata (pureed tomatoes)
2 dried bay leaves
1 teaspoon dried oregano
1 teaspoon ground cinnamon
salt and pepper, to taste

Bechamel

100 g (3½ oz) butter
100 g (⅔ cup) plain (all-purpose) flour
1 litre (4 cups) full-cream (whole) milk
pinch of freshly grated nutmeg
salt and pepper, to taste
1 egg
120 g (1 cup) grated kefalotyri or kasseri cheese (you can also use gruyere), plus extra for sprinkling

Make ahead *Prepare the pastitsio the day before and keep, covered, in the fridge overnight. Once cooked, the pastitsio can also be frozen for up to 2 months.*

Goes with *The Cabbage salad with mint & dried figs on page 157 makes a wonderfully refreshing side to serve with the luscious pastitsio.*

CHARGRILLED PLUMS
WITH HONEY YOGHURT

Cooked plums are sweet and juicy, and when served with a honey and yoghurt dressing, they make an effortless dessert.

✽

Halve the plums and remove the stones, then brush with a little olive oil.

Heat a chargrill pan over medium–high heat, add the halved plums, cut side down, and chargrill for 4–5 minutes, until char lines appear, then turn over and chargrill the other side.

While the plums are cooking, toast the pistachios in a dry frying pan over medium–high heat for 2–3 minutes, until golden around the edges. Remove from the heat and chop roughly.

Place the yoghurt in a large bowl, add the honey and stir to combine.

Spread the honey yoghurt over a serving plate and top with the chargrilled plums. Sprinkle with the cinnamon and toasted pistachios and serve.

Serves 4

4 plums
olive oil, for brushing
120 g (4½ oz) unsalted shelled pistachios
400 g (14 oz) Greek-style yoghurt
2 tablespoons honey
½ teaspoon ground cinnamon

PRICKLY PEAR SORBET

I was on the Greek island of Ikaria when I had my first encounter with the enchanting prickly pear. Juicy and sweet, it was a delicious, unexpected discovery.

Prickly pear's taste can be described as a combination of raspberry and watermelon, and its dense watermelon-like texture makes it an excellent choice for sorbet.

❋

Prepare the prickly pears by wearing kitchen gloves to protect your hands. Peel and cut the pears in half, then scoop out the flesh and set aside.

Place the sugar, lemon juice and 125 ml (½ cup) of water in a saucepan and bring to the boil over medium heat. Reduce the heat to a simmer and cook for 4–5 minutes, until the sugar has dissolved. Remove from the heat and allow to cool.

Place the prickly pear flesh in a blender, add the syrup and puree until smooth. Pour the mixture through a sieve into a shallow dish and place in the freezer for at least 5 hours or overnight.

Scoop the sorbet into bowls and serve.

Serves 4

6 prickly pears, soaked in iced water
   until soft
115 g (½ cup) caster (superfine) sugar
1 tablespoon freshly squeezed
   lemon juice

209

Preparing prickly pears   *Unsurprisingly, prickly pears can be tricky to prepare. I find the best approach is to leave the pears in a bowl of iced water until they are soft enough to easily scrape off the thorns, making them easier and safer to handle.*

BAKED SPICED QUINCE

Quince can be roasted, stewed, pureed, poached, made into jam ... but however it is prepared, this aromatic bright-yellow fruit is nearly always cooked, which changes its colour to a vibrant ruby red.

You can serve this baked spiced quince with vanilla ice cream or Greek-style yoghurt, which is my favourite. It also makes a fantastic accompaniment to cheese.

✽

Preheat the oven to 180°C (350°F) fan-forced.

Heat the butter, honey and 125 ml (½ cup) of water in a flameproof casserole dish (Dutch oven) or large ovenproof frying pan over medium heat until melted and combined. Add the cinnamon stick, nutmeg, allspice and lemon juice.

Peel and cut the quince into quarters, then scoop out the seeds and add the fruit to the dish or pan. Gently stir to coat the quince in the butter and honey mixture, then cover with foil and bake for 1–1½ hours, until the quince turns a deep ruby red and is cooked through.

Serve the roasted quince warm with vanilla ice cream or Greek-style yoghurt, and with the honey-spiced juices drizzled over the top.

Serves 4

100 g (3½ oz) butter
260 g (¾ cup) honey, plus a little
    extra to serve
1 cinnamon stick
½ teaspoon ground nutmeg
¼ teaspoon ground allspice
juice of 1 lemon
4 quince
vanilla ice cream or Greek-style
    yoghurt, to serve

210

APPLE PIE

The aroma of cinnamon and apple baking inspires in me a feeling of cosiness and nostalgia. The flakiness and crunch of the pastry, with the soft chunks of sweet and spicy apple, is one of happiness. This apple pie is one to make on those lazy Sundays ... perhaps even make two and pop one in the freezer for a rainy day.

Serves 4–6

40 g (1½ oz) butter
2 × quantities Flaky pastry, chilled (see page 114)
plain (all-purpose) flour, for dusting
vanilla ice cream or cream, to serve

Apple & cinnamon filling

5 cooking apples
80 g (⅓ cup) caster (superfine) sugar
zest and juice of ½ lemon
1 teaspoon ground cinnamon

Glaze

1 egg yolk
40 g (1½ oz) caster (superfine) sugar

To make the apple and cinnamon filling, peel, core and cut the apples into chunks. Transfer the apple to a large frying pan, along with the sugar and lemon zest and juice, and bring to a simmer over medium heat. Cook for 10–12 minutes, until the sugar has dissolved, then stir through the cinnamon and continue to cook for 4–6 minutes, until the apple has softened a little but is still holding its shape. Remove the pan from the heat and set aside to cool.

Grease a 26 cm (10¼ in) round pie dish with the butter. Remove the pastry from the fridge and divide into two, one piece a little larger than the other.

On a lightly floured work surface, roll out the larger piece of pastry to a circle just bigger than the pie dish. Lay the pastry in the dish and pour in the cooled apple filling. Roll out the remaining pastry into a circle large enough to cover the filling, then place on top of the apple. Trim the edges and pinch or roll to secure.

Whisk together the egg yolk and 1 tablespoon of water in a small bowl. Brush the egg wash over the pastry and sprinkle with the caster sugar.

Bake the apple pie for 45–50 minutes, until golden.

Serve warm with vanilla ice cream or cream.

Make ahead *Uncooked apple pie will keep in a freezer bag in the freezer for up to 3 months. When you are ready to bake, unwrap and bake the pie while still frozen – this will prevent a soggy pie and give you a crisp base.*

MELOPITA

Melopita is a traditional honey cake originating from
the Greek island of Sifnos. If you are a fan of baked
cheesecake, you will love this dessert. I have topped it with
honey-roasted pears for extra indulgence, but you can use
any fruit that's in season or omit it entirely, if you prefer.

❀

Preheat the oven to 180°C (350°F) fan-forced. Grease a 20 cm
(8 in) tart tin and line a baking tray with baking paper.

In a large bowl, whisk together the honey, ricotta, eggs,
vanilla extract and lemon zest until smooth. Pour into the
prepared tin, transfer to the oven and bake for 45 minutes
or until set and golden.

Meanwhile, slice the pears in half and place them
on the prepared tray. Brush with a little honey and roast for
15–20 minutes, until golden. Allow to cool.

Top the honey cheesecake with the roasted pear, drizzle
with a small amount of extra honey and dust with the cinnamon.

Serve warm or at room temperature.

Serves 4

175 g (½ cup) honey, plus extra
    for brushing and drizzling
700 g (1 lb 9 oz) ricotta
4 eggs
1 teaspoon natural vanilla extract
zest of 1 lemon
2 pears
½ teaspoon ground cinnamon

215

CHOCOLATE & FIG TART

I have so many precious memories from my childhood of eating figs picked straight from the tree. I think they might be my favourite fruit – I love them fresh, dried, in salads and, of course, in desserts. Here I've paired figs with dark chocolate to create a rustic tart whose few ingredients belies its rich and complex flavour.

Hot water pastry is one of the easiest pastries you can make and it is suitable for both sweet and savoury tarts. Similar to choux, both the water and fat need to be hot when added to the flour, unlike most pastries where chilling is required. The key is to then shape the pastry into the tart tin while the dough is still warm and flexible.

❉

Preheat the oven to 200°C (400°F) fan-forced.

To make the hot water pastry, place the olive oil, butter, sugar, salt and 80 ml (⅓ cup) of water in a saucepan over medium heat and bring almost to the boil. Remove the pan from the heat, pour in the sifted flour and stir with a wooden spoon until a smooth dough forms.

Tip the dough onto a work surface and lightly knead for 1–2 minutes – it will still be very warm and soft to the touch. Transfer the dough to a 22 cm (8¾ in) round tart tin with a loose base and use your fingers to press the dough evenly to the edge and up the side of the tin.

Bake the tart shell for 12–14 minutes, until golden and cooked through.

Pour the cream into a saucepan and heat gently over low heat. Add the chocolate and stir until melted, then turn the heat off, add the egg and stir well to incorporate completely – the mixture should look silky.

Pour the chocolate filling into the prepared tart crust and smooth the surface with the back of a spoon. Arrange the figs on top, then transfer to the oven and bake for 15 minutes or until the chocolate has set. Allow to cool slightly.

Cut the tart into slices and serve warm or at room temperature with cream.

Serves 6

250 ml (1 cup) pure cream, plus extra
  to serve
200 g (7 oz) good-quality dark
  chocolate (70% cocoa solids),
  broken into pieces
1 egg, beaten
6 figs, thickly sliced

Hot water pastry

1 tablespoon olive oil
90 g (3 oz) unsalted butter
1 tablespoon sugar
pinch of salt
150 g (1 cup) plain (all-purpose) flour,
  sifted

Make ahead   *You can make the tart crust a day in advance and keep it in an airtight container in the fridge overnight.*

BERGAMOT SPOON SWEET

Spoon sweets are usually served with a glass of cold water and a coffee as an act of hospitality in Greece and around the Mediterranean. I love these traditions and recipes that are handed down to the next generation, mother to daughter. There are many varieties, including grape, orange, cherry, quince, fig and watermelon peel. I've used bergamot in this recipe as it's very aromatic and a personal favourite. If you can't find them, substitute orange peels instead.

Spoon sweets are also delicious served on top of Greek-style yoghurt, as part of a dessert and alongside a cheeseboard.

✳

Wash the bergamots and scrub well with a very fine grater (this removes some of the bitterness). Using a sharp knife, score the peel into eight wedges and remove carefully, then scrape away the white pith. Roll the peels into tight scrolls and thread them onto a long piece of cotton using a large needle, making a necklace of bergamot peel rolls.

Place the string of fruit in a large saucepan, add enough water to cover, then bring to the boil, reduce the heat to a simmer and cook for about 4 minutes. Drain and repeat this process once more.

In another saucepan, combine the sugar and 625 ml (2½ cups) of water. Bring to a simmer and cook for 10 minutes or until the sugar has dissolved.

Snip the bergamot peel rolls off the cotton and add to the syrup. Simmer for 15 minutes or until the syrup has thickened. Add the lemon juice, then transfer the bergamot peel rolls and syrup to sterilised jars (see page 21) while still hot. Allow to cool overnight, then store in the fridge for up to 6 months.

Makes 1 kg (2 lb 3 oz)

1 kg (2 lb 3 oz) bergamot
    (or thick-skinned oranges)
1 kg (2 lb 3 oz) caster (superfine) sugar
2 tablespoons freshly squeezed
    lemon juice

218

ABOUT THE AUTHOR

Meni Valle was born in Australia to Greek parents. Her rich Greek heritage, coupled with her love for travel and food, inspired her to pursue a career in the kitchen. Meni is a food teacher and cookbook author, and a respected authority on Mediterranean cuisine.

When she is not writing cookbooks, Meni shares her knowledge and passion for Mediterranean food with a focus on Greek cuisine, through cooking classes and culinary tours to Greece, where she loves connecting with locals and discovering new recipes. She also presents regularly at festivals and conferences, and contributes to magazines.

Meni lives with her family in Melbourne, Australia. She is the author of five cookbooks: *My Greek Kitchen* (2011); *My Mediterranean Kitchen* (2012); *Everyday Mediterranean* (2015); *Mediterranean Lifestyle Cooking* (2019); and *Ikaria* (2020), which won the Prix Eugénie Brazier prize for the French edition, published by Hachette France in 2022, an award created to reward cooking books written by women. *The Mediterranean Cook* is her sixth cookbook.

223

THANK YOU

First of all I would like to thank Paul McNally for making this project possible, and a sincere and heartfelt thank you to the team at Smith Street Books, who made this book into something so very special.

To Lucy Heaver, thank you for your vision, support and believing in me. Thank you for helping me with every step, your sound advice, wonderful and detailed editing, which made all the difference, and the many coffees and chats along the way.

To Stephanie Stamatis and Hugh Davison, my wonderful photographers, thank you for your outstanding photos and for capturing my food so genuinely. I'm so grateful to have worked with you on this book; you are both exceptional talents. Stephanie, for your photography direction and food styling, and for always understanding what I was thinking, thank you for your creative inspiration and bringing my vision to life with such care and detail … so much fun!

To Evi-O.Studio, my wonderful book designer, for your creativity and passion – thank you for making this book so beautiful.

To my dear friend Russel Butcher, for rolling up her sleeves, helping in the kitchen and keeping me organised during the photo shoot, always with such encouragement, laughs and love – thank you for everything.

To Tessa Kiros and Emiko Davies, words cannot express my gratitude for your constant support, encouragement, boundless inspiration and lovely words about this book.

To my family – Steven, Mel, Ben, Cate, Rob, Emilio, Bec, Paul, Isy, Lachie, Sarah and Dave – for your constant encouragement, support and love. From the bottom of my heart, thank you for everything.

And finally, a huge thank you to Arthur. I couldn't have done this without you, your bottomless encouragement, positivity, support and love; eating my food and sharing life with me … thank you!

Meni x

INDEX

226

229

Published in 2024 by Smith Street Books
Naarm (Melbourne) | Australia
smithstreetbooks.com

ISBN: 978-1-9227-5487-5

Smith Street Books respectfully acknowledges the Wurundjeri
People of the Kulin Nation, who are the Traditional Owners
of the land on which we work, and we pay our respects to their
Elders past and present.

Publisher: Paul McNally
Managing editor: Lucy Heaver
Art Direction: Evi-O.Studio | Evi O.
Design: Evi-O.Studio | Rekha Dhanaram & Susan Le
Typesetting: Megan Ellis
Photography: Stephanie Stamatis and Hugh Davison
Photo direction and styling: Stephanie Stamatis
Food preparation: Meni Valle
Proofreader: Pamela Dunne
Indexer: Helena Holmgren

Printed & bound in China by C&C Offset Printing Co., Ltd.

Book 311
10 9 8 7 6 5 4 3 2 1